POCKET GUIDE TO
CRYSTALS
AND
GEMSTONES

BY SIRONA KNIGHT

THE CROSSING PRESS
FREEDOM, CALIFORNIA

This book is for Dr. Marcel Vogel, who was a constant inspiration and dear friend.

Copyright © 1998 by Sirona Knight
Cover photograph by Dean Brittingham
Printed in the U.S.A.

For information on bulk purchases or group discounts for this and other Crossing Press titles, please contact our Special Sales Manager at 800/777-1048.

Visit our Web site on the Internet: www.crossingpress.com

Library of Congress Cataloging-in-Publication Data

Knight, Sirona, 1955-
    Pocket guide to crystals and gemstones / by Sirona Knight.
       p. cm. -- (Crossing Press pocket series)
    Includes bibliographical references.
    ISBN 0-89594-947-4 (pbk.)
    1. Crystals. 2. Precious stones. I. Title. II. Series.
QD905.2.K64   1998
133--dc21
                                98-26906
                                CIP

Table of Contents

Introduction 5

Crystal and Gemstone Basics .6
    What is a Gemstone? 8
    What is a Crystal? 9
    Energy Fields of Crystals and Gemstones 11

Choosing Crystals and Gemstones 15
    Where to Find Crystals and Gemstones 15
    How to Select Personal Stones 17
    Types of Quartz Crystals .19
    Natural, Polished, Cut, and Synthetic Stones 21

Care and Programming of Crystals and Gemstones 23
    Cleaning and Clearing 23
    Salt and Water 24
    Smudging 25
    Pulsing Technique 25
    De-magnetizing Devices .27
    Amplifying 27
    Charging and Programming Crystals 28
    Elemental and Sensory Charging Techniques 30

Traditional Uses 33
    Scrying 34
    Shamanic and Priestly Tools 36
    Birthstones 39
    Sacred Sites and Sacred Stones 40

Contemporary Uses 44
    Pendulums 44
    Wands 46
    Jewelry 47
    Feng Shui 51
    Dreaming 53

Healing Uses 57
    Crystal Healing 57
    Gemstone Essences 59
    Self-Healing Techniques 60
    Treating Common Ailments 61
    Chakra Balancing and Layouts 63
    Marcel Vogel Healing Technique 67

Grids, Gazing, and Ritual 73
    Crystal Grids 73
    Crystal Gazing 80
    Ritual and Ceremony 81

Healing and Spiritual Properties of Crystals
    and Gemstones 84
    List of Stones 84

Introduction

Many people today are rediscovering the sacred and power-ful properties of crystals and gemstones for adornment, health, healing, and spiritual practice. Whether you are newly curious about the different types of stones or want to explore their many ancient and contemporary uses, this book pro-vides a comprehensive overview of the topic. I've included examples of crystal and gemstone use in history and legend, theory of how crystals work, practical applications, and a list-ing of the healing and spiritual properties of over fifty stones.

Beginning with the basic physical and energetic aspects of crystals and gemstones, I provide important information about choosing and caring for stones while remaining respect-ful of their natural origins. Through clear, step-by-step instruc-tions, you will learn how to clean, clear, amplify, and program crystals and gemstones for specific esoteric, healing, ritual, and spiritual uses from different traditions. I hope this book will serve as a useful and continuing reference for your begin-ning to advanced exploration of crystals and gemstones.

Crystal and Gemstone Basics

Grown during the cooling, formative stages of Earth's development, crystals and gemstones are gifts from nature. According to modern physics, they consist of naturally balanced, solid-state energy fields. Because of their energetic properties, crystals and gemstones have a wide range of technological, scientific, and metaphysical uses.

Many cultures around the world, including Chinese, Native American, and Celtic, have traditionally revered and used crystals and gemstones as tools for healing and spiritual purposes. Mythology and history abound with accounts of stones being used in myriad ways, from healing common ailments to protecting the wearer. For example, the purple gem amethyst has been purported to protect against intoxication, to have a sobering effect on passions, and to quicken the intellect. Mentioned in Exodus as one of the stones in the twelve-jeweled breastplate worn by the High Priest Aaron, brother of Moses, amethyst is still worn today by bishops in the Catholic church.

Because of their extremely high and exact rates of vibration, crystals and gemstones play important roles in modern technology, ranging from the liquid crystal diodes on our calculators and clocks to the use of diamonds for precision cutting of optical lenses. The technological uses of crystals and gemstones impact almost every facet of our daily lives, with new uses being discovered all the time. Computers, credit cards, fiber-optic phone lines, and laser technology—which enable everything from new surgical techniques to the playing of compact discs—are just a few of the examples.

Crystals and gemstones are both minerals. Minerals are defined as homogeneous, naturally occurring, inorganic solids. As a result of the orderly arrangement of its atoms, each mineral has a composition that can be expressed in a chemical formula, and a characteristic crystalline structure. The atoms which make up minerals and all matter in the universe are in constant motion. This motion affects the physical structure and energetic field of each stone.

A mineral can be a single element, such as gold, or a complex compound of several elements, such as quartz crystal. The distinctive qualities and properties of each mineral are due to its chemical composition and the patterned arrangement of its atoms. A particularly interesting example of this patterning and its effect is the element carbon, which occurs in nature as several minerals, two of which are graphite and diamond. Identical in chemical composition but with different atomic patterns, they are at opposite ends of the hardness scale, with diamonds being the hardest of minerals and graphite being the softest.

Mineral deposits form in three ways: by precipitating out of a low-temperature solution; forming at depth under great heat and pressure; or crystallizing from hot liquids or gases of magmatic origin. How a mineral originates greatly impacts the patterning of its atoms. For example, it takes a tremendous amount of heat and pressure to create a diamond from carbon, whereas the formation of graphite requires very little heat and pressure.

A rock is an aggregate of minerals. Like minerals, rocks form under a variety of conditions. Mineralogists know where and in what types of rock a particular mineral is likely to be found, and what other minerals are likely to occur nearby. An example of this is tourmaline, which is largely found in deposits of the coarse-grained granitic rock, pegmatite.

WHAT IS A GEMSTONE?

The main difference between crystals and gemstones is that gemstones have ornamental value. To mineral collectors, the term "gemstone" has become the commonly accepted name for all ornamental stones of value, eliminating the previous distinction between so-called precious and semi-precious stones.

Three qualities set gemstones apart from other minerals: rarity, durability, and beauty. Many mineral species qualify as gemstones, which are graded by gemologists according to the following characteristics: vividness of color; "fire"; transparency; luster; and hardness. Gemstones are generally free from flaws and therefore prized for their beauty.

A gemstone becomes a gem when it is cut, shaped, and polished for use as an object of adornment. The final form becomes a faceted stone, a cabochon, or a carving. To create a faceted stone, a gemologist cuts the stone with the intention of bringing out its brilliance and sparkle. The cabochon cut emphasizes a stone's color and pattern by polishing it highly until it's rounded or flattened, rather than faceted. This method is often used on star and cat's eye-type gemstones. Carving is a way of working with larger gemstones such as quartz, turquoise, and jade. In this process, carvers sculpt the stones into a variety of shapes, for example, animals, Goddess figures, and cameos.

WHAT IS A CRYSTAL?

The Earth is composed of 85 percent crystal. The word crystal originates from the Greek word *krystallos*, meaning ice. This stems from the early belief that crystals were pieces of ice, frozen so hard they never melted. Indeed, crystals, in particular clear quartz, do look like ice, as one of their primary characteristics is transparency.

Another defining quality of a crystal is geometric regularity and a repeating internal pattern of its atomic structure. This repeating characteristic is referred to as crystal symmetry. If you rotate a crystal on one of its axes in such a way that the same configuration of faces appears more than once during the course of rotation, this is an axis of symmetry. A plane of symmetry is a place on a crystal where, if it were cut in half, each half would be a mirror image of the other. Crystals also have a center of symmetry meaning that every face of the crystal has a similar face lying parallel to it on the other side. This concept is akin to the human body, which also shows symmetry in that all the elements making up the left side are repeated on the right side, i.e., eyes, hands, ears, legs, and so forth.

The structure of a stone and the shape of its external faces and how they relate to one another also define it as a crystal.

Formed from a gaseous, liquid, or molten state in a process called crystallization, crystals are a large classification of stones including topaz, citrine, and fluorite. Some stones, such as diamonds, rubies, and sapphires, are both crystals and gemstones. For a more complete list of crystals and gemstones, refer to the chapter *Healing and Spiritual Properties of Crystals and Gemstones*. Lead, glass, and synthetic crystal are not included in this book because they do not contain the same healing and/or spiritual properties possessed by natural crystals.

Quartz is the most common crystal—it can be found in all classes of rock, under all sorts of conditions, and in all parts of the world. The most notable quartz specimens come from Arkansas in the United States and Brazil in South America.

The occurrence of single crystals is rare; crystals generally occur in groups which have developed together in rock fissures, on flat surfaces known as druses, or in cavities called geodes. Sometimes crystals develop together in clusters, either in contact or actually interpenetrating one another. Additionally, different types of crystals can grow together—for example, white quartz is sometimes the host stone for emerald. A host stone is a mineral or rock that is older than the stones in it.

In the study of crystals and other minerals, certain characteristics determine classification. These include:

- Texture—The surface appearance of a homogeneous rock or mineral aggregate. The degree of crystallization, the size of the crystals, and the shapes made by the interrelationships of the crystals or other components all contribute to the texture of a mineral.
- Hardness—The resistance of a mineral to abrasion or scratching.
- Luster—The surface appearance or the manner in which it reflects light.

Crystals always grow according to simple mathematical laws and fall within six basic systems, or lattices. These are as follows:

- Isometric—Also referred to as the cubic crystal system; these crystals are blocky or ball-like in appearance, with similar, symmetrical faces. Characteristic forms are cubes, octahedrons, and dodecahedrons.

- Tetragonal—Often long and slender, even needle-like, these forms include four-sided prisms, pyramids, and dipyramids.
- Hexagonal—These crystals are prismatic or columnar in the forms of three- or six-sided prisms, pyramids, and rhombohedrons.
- Orthorhombic—These are short, stubby crystals with a diamond-shaped or rectangular cross section.
- Monoclinic—Mostly stubby, these crystals have tilted matching faces at opposite ends, suggesting a distorted rectangle.
- Triclinic—Usually flat, these crystals have sharp edges and contain no right angles on the faces or edges.

ENERGY FIELDS OF CRYSTALS AND GEMSTONES

Throughout the history of humankind crystals, especially quartz, and gemstones have been highly valued by spiritual leaders, healers, and scientists. Plato's writings referred to extensive use of crystals in Atlantis, and Edgar Cayce, famous seer and healer, often used quartz crystals in his work.

Irish mythology tells the tale of Art, son of King Conn, who was placed by the goddess Creide in a chamber of crystal, a place where all the rays of the sun converged. The hero remained in the crystal chamber for a month, after which he had acquired a new strength and energy, enabling him to face the worst of perils. The crystal chamber was basically equivalent to a healing chamber of the sun.

According to legend, Merlin the Magician resided in a crystal cave with the goddess Viviane, where he stayed protected until awakening from his magic sleep.

Now once again, crystals and gemstones are gaining popularity and attention as tools for the twenty-first century, a time of shifting human consciousness and change. Crystals can help activate and facilitate this transformation through their ability to amplify and balance energy fields such as the ones surrounding your body.

We are more than our physical bodies. We also have an energy body that stores information and roams at will each time we release a thought. Physical form in essence is comprised not of matter, but of energy. Everything that exists is an external manifestation of an energy form, a rate of vibration.

Crystals and gemstones have extremely high and exact rates of vibration which can be precisely manipulated to augment, transform, transduce, store, and focus other rates of vibration. Crystals are used for these purposes in communications, computers, optics, laser technology, audio-visual equipment, microcircuits, and in the equipment used for broadcasting radio and television signals. These same vibrational qualities of crystals can be used to modify thoughts, emotions, and the energy fields of human bodies and other physical forms by first effecting change on the subtle energetic level—just as shamans, healers, and mystics have been doing for ages.

Crystals restore balance in your body, allowing your body to breathe again in a meaningful and harmonious way. All life, in order to exist and be meaningful, must be in a state of balance. When life becomes polarized in one direction or the other, there is an imbalance and interference with the natural pattern of living. Quartz crystals, blood, and water all have an affinity for each other because they all share common elemental properties.

Crystals store energy, a certain rate of vibration, a specific matrix structure, color, memories, as well as sound, fragrance, light, emotions, dreams, and specific experiences. The form and development of quartz crystals is governed by morphogenetic fields. Crystals consist of atoms arranged in a patterned and orderly fashion, and are living entities in their own right. They exhibit a naturally balanced, solid state energy field, which makes them invaluable in electronic equipment. Crystal energy affects our totality like each breath of fresh air.

Quartz crystals have piezoelectric properties, meaning they emit an electrical charge when pressure is applied to them. Piezoelectronics use crystals in radio transmission, sonar equipment, and aircraft frequency control. Crystals also have pyroelectric qualities, meaning they produce an electric charge when heated.

The piezoelectric and pyroelectric properties of crystals are used in: oscillators, which control radio frequencies in electronic equipment; capacitors, which modify energy capacity and block excessive flow; transducers, which transmit energy from one system to another; condensers, which store a continual charge from an energy force field in solid form; energy force fields, used as sonic protection against static, and around an area or individual; and body balancers, which alter the body's vibration or frequency by passing ions through the crystal's molecular structure.

These are the same qualities that allow quartz crystals to modify thought and emotions and to heal our bodies and other physical forms by first effecting changes on a subtle, energetic plane. For example, the basis of crystal healing relies on the principle that disharmonious energy can be harmonized. Crystals and gemstones can amplify and transform thoughts, and increase powers of meditation, intention, visualization, and affirmation.

One early conception of crystals was that they were the living brain cells of the Earth Mother Gaia. If this is true, we are destroying countless cells for use in stereos and computers, as well as objects of adornment and metaphysical tools. As mentioned earlier, crystals and gemstones represent gifts from the Earth, and should be treated as such. When harvesting crystals and stones, please be aware of the finite nature of these gifts, which are often a one-time harvest, being dug up at an ever-increasing rate. Crystals and gemstones, as with anything in nature, represent the eternal connection between human beings and the Earth. As with all relationships, this connection works best when it's in harmony and balance.

Choosing Crystals and Gemstones

WHERE TO FIND CRYSTALS AND GEMSTONES

Finding and purchasing crystals and gemstones is an adventure, often an enjoyable one. Many inexpensive stones are available for those just beginning to collect and use stones, and of course, there are more expensive stones, costing hundreds of thousands of dollars, such as the famed "padparadschah," an extremely rare orange variety of corundum.

Crystals and gemstones are a good investment, not only because of their enduring beauty, but also because of their spiritually nourishing and healing qualities. Many gemstones appreciate in value quickly, depending on the type of stone, the setting, cut, carat weight, and so forth. Keep in mind that the most expensive stone is not necessarily the best stone to use for healing and spiritual purposes.

Stones often come into your possession at a time when you need them—as gifts, through bartering, or by purchasing them. Some of the sources for stones are rock shops; gemstone and mineral shows; New Age stores, fairs, and events; antique, metaphysical, jewelry, or pagan supply stores; gem or rock clubs; mail order catalogs; natural history museums; and even the mines themselves. Don't overlook the possibility of finding beautiful and useful stones, such as quartz and obsidian, while walking in the mountains or along a dry river bed. If the Earth gifts you with a beautiful stone, be sure to give thanks in return.

It is important to know where your stones come from, and by what means they have been excavated from the land. For example, strip mining is the cheapest method of extracting crystals, but also the most damaging to the Earth. When you purchase a crystal obtained in this way, you indirectly condone and participate in the destruction of the Earth, rather than working in harmony with the elements and land.

Although both unfortunate and unwise, many countries are pitting the Earth and stripping the land away for gemstones and crystals in order to meet the incredible market demand. Because most of the stones near the surface have already been mined, mines are now being dug deeper into the Earth. For instance, ten years ago Herkimer diamonds were found just inches below the soil, whereas today miners must dig fifty feet or more to find these same stones. This deeper mining costs more, which is reflected in the escalating prices of crystals and gemstones.

When selecting personal stones, ask the salesperson all the questions you feel are pertinent to buying and using the stone. If you don't like any of the answers you receive, perhaps you should find a different source for stones. Buying a crystal or gemstone should be a positive experience, and never rushed or forced.

The following list provides tips on what to look for when purchasing crystals and gemstones:

- Damage—the less damage (imperfections, cracks, chips) the better. Chipped tips on quartz crystals are the worst sort of damage.
- Clarity—Depending on the type of stone, clarity is usually a desired characteristic, especially in clear quartz. Clear points, which are very clear quartz crystal points, make excellent pendants, healing tools, and wands.

- Shape and configuration—Odd and unusual shapes cost more, for example, tabbies, which are flat healing crystals.
- Rarity—When particular mines close or the mineral becomes scarce, the cost escalates. Rare stones are the most costly.
- Inclusions—The rainbows, patterns, or landscapes inside the stone that are desirable for various ritual and ceremonial uses.
- Spiritual Qualities—Generators, healing crystals, record keepers, meditation, and channeling stones used for esoteric, meditation, and energy applications. See "Types of Quartz Crystals" and "Healing and Spiritual Properties of Crystals and Gemstones."

HOW TO SELECT PERSONAL STONES

All crystals and stones are naturally tuned to particular frequencies, vibrations, and harmonics of energy. When you are in attunement with a stone, you will experience sensations of balance, harmony, clarity, and wholeness.

Choosing stones is an intuitive act. Take a deep breath and notice which stones feel good to you. If a stone feels right, it's probably the right one for you. If it doesn't feel right, try another one.

To increase your sensitivity to the energies of crystals and gemstones, first wash your hands, dry them completely, and rub them together vigorously and rapidly several times to build up a surface charge. Pick up the crystal or gemstone and feel the energy. Your hand may actually stick to the stone. This indicates that you and the stone are in harmony.

One effective means for selecting personal stones is simplified kinesiology. Working with another person, extend your right arm at shoulder height. With your left hand, hold the crystal or stone on your witness area at the thymus, where your physical and subtle energy bodies meet, and ask the question, "Is this a good stone for me to use, wear, or carry?" Continue by asking for more specific information, such as, "Is this a good stone for me to use for healing? For meditation? For channeling?" After each question, have the other person press down firmly on your extended arm, while you resist. If your arm remains strong, you have made a wise selection. If your arm becomes weak, choose another stone.

Another way to test how "in sync" you are with a particular crystal is by holding the crystal in your right hand and drawing in a deep breath. Hold your breath until you feel your body vibrate or oscillate. As you exhale and relax, point the tip of the crystal (the dominant tip, if it is double terminated—see page 19) toward the palm of your left hand, and at a distance of five to nine inches, begin to move the crystal slowly up and down. You should feel a tingling sensation in your left hand, reflecting the movements of the crystal. The feeling you experience may be akin to a slight breeze flowing across the surface of your skin. First, move your hands closer together, and then about an arm's length apart, all the while noticing the difference in the sensations from the crystal. The stronger the tingling sensation or breeze, the stronger your connection with that particular crystal.

As you work with crystals and gemstones, you may experience or intuit a variety of sensations. Following is a list of examples:

- Tingling or energetic charge in your hands or across your skin
- Electric charge or humming sensation
- Sweating or dampness, a slickness when rubbing the stone
- Heat
- Cold
- Vibration or pulsing

- Flow of energy or heat from the crystal tip
- Twitching in your fingers and thumbs
- Breeze or cool wind across your skin
- Sound or audible humming in your ears
- Glowing light or a visible or sensed field of energy
- Scent or odor
- Immediate sense of balance and being centered

TYPES OF QUARTZ CRYSTALS

Attunement Crystals—These serve as "tuning forks'" in meditation, influence and increase the vibration of energy within a certain sphere or area, and key to specific harmonics of energy. They are usually very clear and simple.

Cluster—A group of connected crystals usually joined at the base. One or more crystals growing from the same host stone.

Crystal Pairs—Twinned crystals, used for uniting energies and communicating with the divine.

Dead Crystals—Irradiated stones that are vibrationally dead and therefore useless. Most smoky quartz sold in the U.S. is white or clear quartz from Arkansas that has been irradiated. When purchasing stones, don't hesitate to ask the salesperson where the stones come from, and if they've been treated in any way. Look for genuine smokies from Nevada, California, Washington, and Montana.

Devic Crystals—Elemental devas use crystals as dwelling places. These crystals are usually formed in such a way as to allow entrance into the stone. Best kept in a special, secluded spot, and used primarily for multidimensional communication and travel.

Double-terminated—A crystal with two points, one on each end. Energy moves in both directions in these stones, but usually one of the points is dominant, meaning it projects more energy than the opposite end.

Fire Crystals—Intense energy crystals that seem to radiate a fire from within, and act as a long-lasting source of energy.

Generator—A large quartz, hand-sized or larger, used to generate energy. Often used in crystal grids (see page 71) or to create ley lines, which are energetic lines that crisscross the Earth's surface.

Generator Cluster—A very large group of connected crystals, used to generate great amounts of energy. Excellent for manifesting goals and ideas.

Geode—A hollow stone, lined on the inside with crystals. Also crystals layered on the top and bottom of a stone.

Goddess Crystal—Quartz crystals with a five-sided C-face (located on the tip, this is the largest of the crystal's six faces). Two sides are longer and form an arrow point.

Healing Crystals—Usually palm-sized crystals that exhibit a balanced field of energy, and elicit a like response of harmony when employed for treating imbalances in the body.

Hydro Crystals—Quartz with one or more water bubbles. The trapped water is hundreds of thousands to millions of years old. Adding the elemental quality of water is extremely useful in healing, due to the fact that the human body is mostly made up of water.

Penetrator—A crystal that grows through and extends out of a larger crystal. These are ritual and ceremonial stones of initiation and rebirth.

Library Crystals—Stones with the capacity to receive and store large amounts of information. Very useful when learning, studying, or doing research work. Often these crystals already have a great deal of knowledge embedded in them. These crystals feel very dense or heavy and often have multiple pyramids and windows in them.

Phantom—An image within the quartz, created by inclusions, that echoes the shape of the outer crystal. Excellent stones for healing.

Rainbows—Inclusions within a quartz crystal that resemble a rainbow when the crystal is placed in the sun or under a bright light. Used for meditation, crystal gazing, and ritual. Double rainbows are very rare and particularly useful for out-of-body, shapeshifting, and channeling work.

Record Keepers—Crystals with three-sided pyramids which are within the stone, etched into it, or raised above its surface. Considered to carry the wisdom of the ancients.

Power Rods—Long, thin crystals that respond quickly and powerfully to thought-forms and project them in a laser-like beam of energy. Used to motivate change.

Reverse-sceptered—A crystal with a small, fine, and delicate tip, and a larger stone at its base.

Ritual Crystals and Gemstones—Consecrated stones such as initiation pendants and talismans, used primarily for ritual.

Sceptered Crystal—Quartz with a primary crystal and another crystal growing on the tip.

Scrying Crystals—Usually large quartz crystals with very clear centers. Often spheres, pyramids, obelisks, and similarly shaped quartz crystals are used for scrying (see page 31) or crystal gazing (see page 75).

Singing Crystals—Stones that seem to sound when they are used in certain applications, such as meditation, healing, or ritual.

Skeletal Quartz—Stones with small openings and channels into the layered interior. These crystals work especially well for communicating with angels, ancestors, and otherworldly beings.

Transmitting Crystals—Quartz that transmit a wide spectrum of spiritual light, which serve as tools to amplify and project thought-forms or light from place to place.

Watchtower Crystals—Very clear, single-terminated and fine-pointed quartz crystals that are tuned in a specific manner and used exclusively for guarding the Four Corners: North, East, South, and West. (See the chapter on "Ritual and Ceremony.")

NATURAL, POLISHED, CUT, AND SYNTHETIC STONES

The energetic and healing effects of a stone differ depending on whether it is polished and cut or in its natural state. Certain stones need cutting and polishing to bring out their properties, while others work better in their raw, uncut state. Some healers work primarily with polished stones, while others feel natural stones, or a combination of polished and natural stones, work best. Use your own intuition and judgment when choosing a polished, cut, or natural stone. The stones you are drawn to are probably the most appropriate ones. Cut and polished stones are usually more expensive than natural stones.

In general, gemstones transmit their energies more intensely when polished, while clear quartz remains very powerful both in its natural and cut state. Cutting and polishing an amethyst crystal often increases its energy and effects. Also, garnet and ruby are highly effective when cut and set properly in jewelry.

Unlike natural stones, synthetic crystals are not beneficial for healing or energy balancing. Simulated gemstones do not contain all of the elements found in natural stones. Because they are grown in the laboratory they do not interact with your body's energy in the same way as natural stones, and are solely attuned to the person(s) who manufactured them. Worthless for purposes of therapy and healing, I do not recommend using simulated gemstones or crystals for anything but occasional adornment—but be sure not to allow synthetic stones to touch your skin. Also avoid using all irradiated and heat-treated stones, as they can be harmful and are definitely useless for healing or spiritual applications.

Care and Programming of Crystals and Gemstones

CLEANING AND CLEARING

Crystals and gemstones constantly collect energy from their surrounding environment. This build-up is a record of the energy of each person who has come in contact with the stone.

Whenever you obtain a new crystal or gemstone, clean and clear the stone before using it. Cleaning the stone is crucial when you use it for healing and spiritual work. This is particularly important if you use someone else's crystal: if you do not clear it first, instead of getting a clear channel you will pick up the other person's vibration. By using the cleaning and clearing methods outlined in this chapter, you will be assured of starting with a clear energetic channel, using your crystals and gemstones to their fullest spiritual and healing potential.

Following are some tips for physically cleaning your stones:

- A soft toothbrush or vegetable brush is good for loosening dirt particles, particularly when cleaning clusters.
- Avoid soaking stone clusters, geodes, and soft stones, as they can break apart and crumble.
- Keep crystals and stones in a container or a natural cloth bag between cleanings.
- Do not click the stones together as you clean them because they will chip and crack.
- Avoid extreme temperatures and sudden changes of temperature when cleaning stones. This can crack them, particularly if a weak point exists in the stone.

- Use soap only as a last resort, and use only natural soaps and detergents, nothing synthetic.
- Be aware of magnetic fields, EMF fields, and polarities within your house as these will change the resonance in the stones.

SALT AND WATER

One simple method for purifying the energy in a crystal or gemstone is to use salt. Traditionally, metaphysicians used salt to break up energetic patterns, because the crystals of salt absorb and clear the energy of everything that comes into contact with them. When using salt for clearing your crystals, use natural sea salt rather than salt processed with chemicals. Follow these steps for using dry salt to clear the energy in your crystals and gemstones:

1. Fill a container large enough to hold your crystal with dry salt.
2. Put the crystal into the container, submerging it completely in the salt.
3. After a few minutes, remove the crystal from the salt, and hold it in your hand. Use your intuition to check into the crystal. The energy field should feel cleaner.
4. Dispose of the used salt—do not use it, either in your salt shaker or bath.

In the case of stones which have had major energy patterns imprinted in them, you may need to use this technique in conjunction with other clearing methods to ensure that the crystal is indeed free of unwanted energy. Some experts suggest that the crystal be packed in salt for twenty-four to forty-eight hours. This isn't necessary, because as soon as the crystal makes contact with the salt, the energy is transferred.

Another method is to place the stone in salt water for a few minutes to twenty-four hours. I have found that a few minutes is sufficient, and that leaving stones in longer pits them or breaks them apart. Another quick way to clear your stone is by holding it under cold running water for a minute, tip downward, and visualizing white light washing through it.

SMUDGING

Smudging is a traditional cleansing technique used primarily by Native American shamans. They use the smoke of certain herbs, including sage, cedar, and sweet grass, to purify their bodies and lodges. The purpose of smudging crystals is essentially the same. The smoke of the herbs cleanses the energy of the stone.

Smudge sticks made of these herbs can be found in metaphysical or New Age stores, and are reasonably priced; or you can collect and dry your own sage, cedar, and sweet grass. You can also smudge your stones with sandalwood incense, or copal, a resin, which have a purifying effect on energy. Following is a basic method for smudging your crystals and gemstones:

1. Light the smudge stick or incense, and blow on it softly until it starts to smoke. Hold a fireproof dish or container under the burning smudge, as pieces of the burning herbs may drop off.
2. Take the crystal in your hand and pass it through the smoke, making sure the smoke completely surrounds it.
3. Continue moving the crystal through the smoke until it feels clean to you. The number of times you need to pass the crystal through the smoke depends on the strength of the energetic charge in the crystal. As always, trust your intuition when smudging your stones.

PULSING TECHNIQUE

The pulsing method uses breath and intention to clear the stone. Breath is the staff of life, while intention forms the foundation of all spiritual and healing work. Cradle the crystal or stone between the thumb and middle or index finger of your left hand; place the thumb and index or middle finger of your right hand on either end of the crystal or stone. By using both hands, you create a flow of energy, or natural circuit. When working with spheres, clusters, or similarly shaped stones, simply cup the stone between the palms of your hands, with your right hand on top.

Your intention is one of clearing; hence in your mind's eye visualize an image, or sense a feeling of clearing or clarity filling the crystal or stone. As you breathe in deeply, visualize whatever symbolizes clarity to you, and then pulse your breath out, sharply through your nostrils only, not your mouth. Your pulsed breath becomes a carrier wave for the image or sensation of clearing that occupies your awareness as you breathe out.

Dr. Marcel Vogel taught me several ways to clear crystals. Dr. Vogel was one of IBM's most prolific Senior Scientists, with over 100 patents in his name. He was a man of unlimited creativity and faith, who was recognized as an authority on the therapeutic use of crystals. One helpful method for clearing crystals is to breathe in and visualize or sense a laser beam of white light moving from your forehead or third eye to the stone. As you pulse your breath out, fill the stone with cleansing light. Another useful method is to breathe in and visualize or sense a black void with a single point of white light in the center. Place this image into the crystal or stone with your pulsed breath.

Rotate the crystal or stone in your hands as many times as you feel necessary for thorough clearing, repeating the pulsing technique each time. In this manner, you clear the major axes and faces of the crystal or stone.

The pulsing technique effectively clears crystals, stones, and metals, which makes this technique particularly useful for jewelry, healing crystals, and pendulums, as well as crystal and stone tools. Personal jewelry that is worn regularly should be cleared at least once a day, and any stones used for healing, meditation, or divination need to be cleared immediately after the work is finished. By pulsing, you can return jewelry, crystals, and gemstones to their normal vibrational state, ridding them of any residual energy or undesired charge.

DE-MAGNETIZING DEVICES

Another method for clearing crystals and gemstones is by using a de-magnetizer or bulk eraser. These devices are available at most electronic supply and stereo stores. In much the same way that you would use it to de-magnetize tape heads, draw the de-magnetizer along the outer edges and faces of the stone to erase any unwanted energy or residual charge. Cover each face.

There is a great deal of speculation about the desirability of using electronic devices to clear crystals and stones. This method of clearing is my least favorite, but it is effective and practical for clearing a large number of stones in a short period of time. Used in tandem with salt water, de-magnetizing devices are very effective.

AMPLIFYING

Holding the crystal in your right hand, with the tip pointed outward, snap your wrist in a whipping motion, directing the energy of the crystal into the ground. This motion stimulates the crystal into full activity. If you visualize cobalt blue light flowing through the crystal while doing this, it also has the effect of clearing the stone. Because the motion is easy and quick, this method is especially effective during healing procedures, when the stone builds up negative energy. Be sure to point your crystal toward the ground. In this way, any unwanted energy is absorbed and transformed by the earth.

CHARGING AND PROGRAMMING CRYSTALS

Crystals act as simple computers and can be tuned and programmed to your vibration. Through this vibration, you communicate—receive and send—a charge from another person or object. Just by holding a stone, you charge or imprint it with your energy. You can store any pattern of thought that you choose in your crystal. For example, if you want to expand your awareness, place that thought-form into the stone, and carry it on your person. This process is a simple way to access and develop your personal abilities, such as concentration, healing, meditation, relaxation, and goal achievement.

Intention and breath are the key components in charging and programming crystals. Your indwelling breath diminishes the charge, while your outgoing breath amplifies it. The ideal intention when working with crystals and stones is one of love and well-being. By directing your intention and breath in specific ways, you set up a vibrational field or charge within the crystal. This transfer charge is stored within the crystalline lattice, and carries a magnetic quality that can be erased, just as it can be programmed.

The programming procedure is simple. While holding your cleared crystal in your right hand, point it toward the palm of your left hand, at a distance of eight to twelve inches. Close your eyes, take a deep breath and hold it a few moments. At the same time, focus your attention and awareness on the tip of the crystal. Visualize and verbalize what program you wish to put into the crystal. As you exhale, sharply pulse your breath through your nostrils, not your mouth. This transfers your feelings and visual messages to the crystal. Repeat this procedure three times for a six-sided crystal, cluster, or sphere, four times for an eight-sided crystal.

This charging or programming process links the crystal to the vibration of your body. Every living form has its personal vibration, like a signature. The rhythmic vibration of the crystal, which resonates with the vibration of your etheric body (your subtle energy body that surrounds you), is similar to your heartbeat, but much faster and more delicate.

The strength of the crystal charge or program depends on your level of concentration and clarity of intent. Staying focused on the task at hand is the key to crystal programming. If you find your mind wandering, stop what you are doing and regain your center and focus. Take a deep breath and turn your mind to oneness, which will help you to regain your focus.

Your breathing acts as a carrier wave. You program the crystal by imprinting a thought-form onto this carrier wave, which is absorbed by the stone. Thought is rhythmic energy, and displays distinct repeating patterns. When you program a crystal with specific thought patterns, the stone reflects this pattern when you use it in any application, be it healing, meditation, prophecy, protection, or astral projection.

To check if your crystal is charged and programmed, rub one of the faces with your index or middle finger. You should feel it stick slightly to the crystal. It may feel as if the crystal is sweating or vibrating.

The crystal will hold the charge or program until you clear it or reprogram it. For this reason, clearing and cleaning your crystals after you use them is standard procedure. Otherwise you remain connected to the crystal and any energies that permeate or influence it.

You can charge crystals with a permanent program. For instance, the crystal you wear can be programmed with a non-erasable program of love, well-being, and protection. To do this, simply clear the crystal and then charge it with that program, first along one axis, then along a second axis at right angles, and finally along the third axis, creating a three-dimensional program. To check whether the program is indeed permanent, try clearing the crystal in the usual ways, and see if the program remains. If it does, go ahead and repeat the procedure to reinforce the original program.

Once you have set the primary program in place, you can then imprint the crystal with secondary programs, depending on its use and your intention. Remember, your intention is what is most important. Don't be overly concerned with whether your crystal is perfectly charged and programmed. The depth of your connection with the crystal determines its effectiveness.

ELEMENTAL AND SENSORY CHARGING TECHNIQUES

You can charge crystals and gemstones with the natural energy of the four elements—earth, air, fire, and water, as well as with sound and light. The following are ways of charging your stones with the energies of nature.

Sunlight: Place the crystal outside in the sun, on a fireproof surface. Avoid setting clear stones on the window sill, as they magnify the sun's rays and can actually burn a hole in the sill, and possibly start a fire. Depending on the charge you want to put in the crystal, you may want to set it out several days in a row until the sun's energy is firmly lodged within it. If you want only the sun's energy in the crystal, remember to bring it in each day before the sun goes down, otherwise moon and star energy will also be imparted to the stone. Never place your crystals or stones in fire, as this will damage them, both physically and energetically.

Moonlight: One method for charging your crystal with moonlight involves placing the crystal out at night for an entire cycle of the moon (twenty-eight days). Another method is to leave the crystal out only during the full moon, new moon, crescent moon, and so forth, depending on the kind of energy you want it to absorb.

Starlight: I suggest you try this technique on a New Moon because the stars are much more visible. Also if possible, select a spot on the beach, the mountains, or in the desert where there are no extraneous lights. Begin with a cleared stone. Select a favorite star in the night sky, for example Sirius. Stare or gaze at the star while holding your crystal or gemstone cradled in both hands. Slowly lift the stone in front of you with your left hand until the light from Sirius shines through it. Gaze at the crystal absorbing the star energy for about five minutes, and then switch the crystal to your right hand. Allow the starlight to shine through it for five more minutes. Use your breath to pulse the light and qualities of the star into your stone. This charging technique works best with clear quartz crystals because of their clarity and ability to absorb light.

Earth, sand, soil: Bury the crystal or gemstone in the earth, sand, or soil. The longer you leave it buried, the stronger the charge. Leaving the stone in the earth for a full year is particularly effective, as the natural seasonal cycle becomes embedded in it. If you have a favorite spot out in nature, bury the stone there. It will collect the energy from the site, and you can tap into this energy when using or carrying the stone.

Air, incense, oils: Place your stones outside during a strong wind to charge them with the element of air. Burn incense and pass your stones through the smoke. Sandalwood, copal resin, sweet grass, and pine smoke are particularly useful, and can also clean any negative energy from stones. To charge your stones with oil essences, place one drop on the tip of the crystal. Stones may become gummed up with oil, so be sure to clean them with a sea salt solution after use.

Water, ocean, lakes, rivers: Submerge the crystal in the water of the ocean, lake, or river having the energy you want to impart to the crystal. The longer you leave the crystal in the water, the longer the charge will last.

Sound charging: Use music, chanting, singing, drumming, and other sounds to enhance the healing or spiritual properties of your crystals and gemstones. One way of doing this is to place your stones next to your stereo speakers.

Traditional Uses

For the purposes of this book, the spiritual and metaphysical uses of crystals and gemstones are delineated into traditional and contemporary uses. However, many traditional uses, such as scrying, are still practiced today, and many contemporary uses, such as crystal wands, stem from traditions handed down through generations.

The reason for separating the uses of crystals and gemstones into traditional and contemporary is due to the modern perception of crystals and gemstones as ancient stones as well as building blocks for much of modern technology. Because of this perception, uses such as scrying, which is an ancient fortune-telling method, have a more traditional feel to them, whereas the use of pendulums and crystal wands have gained popularity for contemporary use today. For this reason, the use of crystals and gemstones in scrying, ancient shamanic tools, and sacred sites is presented in this chapter, and the practices of using stones in pendulums, wands, jewelry, feng shui, and dreaming are covered in the next chapter.

Stones had practical uses for the ancients, serving as weapons, fortifications, name and date markers, monuments, talismans, and even as implements for creating fire. The early philosophers taught that the four elements were present in the physiology of the human body, with earth corresponding to our bones and flesh. Thus, in esoteric traditions, stones and rocks represented the bones of the Gods and Goddesses.

A rock became the symbol for the body of all things. Eventually this symbolism evolved into the use of cube-shaped rocks for pedestals, while the spiritual essence of all things came to be symbolized by carved figures which surmounted the pedestals. These pedestals and sculpted stones were the first altars and lithic images of deities.

Gemstones and minerals played an important role in the ancient art of alchemy. To the alchemist there are three primary kingdoms—mineral, animal, and vegetable, with each kingdom exhibiting its own essence. All three derive from a common source, but each manifests under different vibrations within its respective realm. The mineral kingdom has the highest vibration. Humankind can partake of these vibrations to our benefit through the art and craft of alchemy.

The elements earth, air, fire, and water, long used in ritual practices, are also related to particular stones. Some elemental correspondences are as follows:

Earth: Agate, Onyx, Obsidian, Rock Quartz, Emerald
Air: Topaz, Opal, Diamond, Zircon
Fire: Ruby, Fire Opal, Carnelian, Garnet
Water: Moonstone, Aquamarine, Azurite, Lapis Lazuli

SCRYING

Also called crystallomancy, scrying is a technique used by seers, psychics, and sorcerers. Using crystals and gemstones in the divination of one's past, present, and future traditionally played a key role in decision-making for powerful leaders throughout history, including King Arthur, who sought out the advice and prophecies of Merlin the Magician, and Queen Elizabeth I, who at times consulted the famous seventeenth-century scryer, Dr. Dee, on matters of state.

One of the earliest and best-known forms of divination, scrying began with the use of reflective surfaces to gain knowledge about the future. One of the earliest uses of crystals and gemstones in scrying was by the druids, who used beryl crystals. Scottish Highlanders called these "stones of power." The earliest crystal balls were made of beryl, and were later replaced by spheres made from rock crystal. Prominent in the middle ages, scryers revered their crystal balls, and often passed them on to their apprentices.

Many other cultures around the world have traditionally used crystals and gemstones for scrying. Examples include the diviners of the Yucatan, who revered clear stones such as quartz, and Apache medicine men, who used crystals for inducing visions.

Divination is a tool for reaching and communicating with the *divine*, which implies that crystals have always been used in communications, just as they are today in radios, telephones, and computers. The reason crystals in particular became important tools for scrying is because of their inherent characteristics of transparency and regularity of patterns, called symmetry. Additionally, the energetic fields of crystals and gemstones influence what the scryer sees on a very subtle and often esoteric level.

Use the following basic technique as a guide for your own crystal scrying, adapting the procedure to your own needs. Remember to trust your intuition.

Begin by selecting a stone which refracts light well and that is mostly clear, and feels physically and psychically comfortable to you. Once you've chosen a stone for scrying, clear it out using the steps outlined in the section on cleaning and clearing (see page 23). Once cleared, the crystal can be used as it is or charged with energy before using it to scry. Traditionally, scrying stones and spheres were never exposed to sunlight because this was thought to hinder their ability to connect and communicate with the psychic mind and the divine. However, moonlight enhanced this ability; the full moon is the best time to charge your scrying crystal with moon energy. (See page 31 for a complete explanation and step-by-step instructions for charging stones with moonlight.)

Seven Steps for Crystal Scrying:

1. Scrying works best at night because night rules the psychic mind. Find a quiet spot, sit comfortably, and place the crystal on a stand or table, or hold it in your hands.

2. Candles are conducive to scrying. If you find yourself distracted by the reflections and movements of the flame, then experiment by using other light sources, or move the candle until you find what works for you.

3. Relax by breathing deeply for a few moments with your eyes closed.

4. Open your eyes and hold the crystal in your hands until it is warm. Many scryers say this is important for connecting your energy to that of the stone. Heating the stone also activates it.

5. While holding the stone, think about your intentions. For example, you might be seeking information about your career, relationship, or future. Be clear about your intention.

6. Next, place the stone back in its resting place or continue holding it in your hands, and begin gazing into it.

7. As you gaze deeply into the crystal, move your mind beyond the physical structure of the stone, merging into the light within. The idea is not so much to see physical images, but to use the crystal and the light reflecting in it to help you connect to the divine energy within yourself and all things. When connected, you should begin getting impressions and insights. Practice this technique, merging with the crystal, until everything flows and feels comfortable to you.

SHAMANIC AND PRIESTLY TOOLS

All around the world, shamanic and spiritual masters traditionally used crystals and gemstones as tools for finding answers to esoteric questions such as the meaning of life. Early in their pursuit, they discovered the curative properties of crystals and gemstones. An example of this is the British folk belief that quartz crystals, highly prized for their curative properties, were "star-stones" and gifts from the celestial skies. Healers collected nine star-stones from a running brook, and then boiled them in a quart of water from the same brook. This process imparted the healing power of the stones to the water, which was then given to a patient for nine successive mornings.

Throughout the world, quartz crystals have been associated with shamanic practices. Shamans consider them to be pieces of solidified light, which serve as bridges across the thresholds of Earth into other dimensions of existence. They use quartz and other crystals as a catalyst and a rainbow bridge to these other worlds.

In some traditions, shamanic initiates receive crystals as part of their rite of passage, in which they die to their earthly bodies in order to be reborn into the adamantine "crystal body" or "light body." During this rite, crystals are swallowed, or abraded and rubbed in a paste on the initiate's skin, or placed under a fingernail or under their tongues.

Shamans also perceive crystals to be living beings, and use them as power objects, or spirit helpers. The Jivro shaman of the Amazon keeps a crystal in his power bag as does the Paipai shaman. The Mexican Huichols believe that the souls of shamans return to the Earth in the form of quartz crystals, and the Warao shamans of South America put quartz crystals in their medicine rattles as spirit helpers to help extract harmful energies.

Quartz is the only power object that remains the same whether the shaman is in a normal waking state or in an altered state of consciousness. In this way, the crystal acts as a window or portal between worlds. The healer is said to see the sickness in the crystal, and the being within the crystal shows the shaman the cause and appropriate treatment.

Other traditional uses of crystals and gemstones include the twelve-jeweled High Priest's breastplate, worn by Aaron, brother of Moses, which consisted of twelve stones, arranged on a silver plate in three vertical rows of four stones. The stones were sard, agate, chrysolite, garnet, amethyst, jasper, onyx, beryl, emerald, topaz, sapphire, and diamond. Of these, amethyst, jasper, onyx, and agate belong to the quartz family. The combination of these minerals created particular vibrations that the high priest could tap into for magical works.

In Western tradition, amethyst crystals have been fashioned into jewelry in the forms of crowns, rings, and broaches, made for royalty and the higher levels of religious hierarchy. In the Catholic church, amethyst is part of the Fisherman's Ring worn by the Pope. The Fisherman's Ring is a signet ring with the name of the Pope encircling a depiction of Saint Peter in a fishing boat. When the Pope dies, the ring is destroyed. As mentioned previously, amethyst is the stone associated with priests and bishops.

The crozier of a Catholic bishop, his pectoral cross, the altar stones, candlesticks, and certain crosses carry seven main stones: diamond or clear quartz, sapphire, jasper, emerald, topaz, ruby, and amethyst. In the Episcopal Cross the amethyst is placed in the middle with the sapphire under it, the diamond above it, and more amethysts placed at the extremities. In other contexts the diamond or clear quartz is placed in the middle of the other stones. The radiations from these groups of precious stones are thought to attract a complete spectrum of spiritual energies.

BIRTHSTONES

Certain crystals and gemstones are identified with the different signs of the zodiac, each stone having unique properties that can be used during particular seasonal cycles, and which bring good fortune and harmony to the wearer. The idea of wearing a specific stone because you were born under that zodiac sign is erroneous, and, for the most part, circulated by the jewelry industry. Rather, birthstones are gateways to the vibrational cycles of the Earth, moon, sun, and stars. The original idea was to collect and use twelve stones throughout the year, one for each sign of the zodiac, for the purposes of exploring the qualities of each sign. Lists of birthstones vary considerably. The tabulation below places the commonly accepted stones next to each of the twelve zodiac signs.

Sun Sign	Gemstone
Aries	Ruby, Bloodstone, Diamond, Sapphire, Garnet, Red Jasper
Taurus	Emerald, Carnelian, Agate, Golden Topaz, Lapis Lazuli, Alexandrite
Gemini	Aquamarine, Rock Quartz, Agate, Alexandrite, Chrysoberyl
Cancer	Emerald, Moonstone
Leo	Ruby, Cat's Eye, Carnelian, Onyx, Citrine, Heliodor
Virgo	Zircon, Sapphire, Pink Jasper, Rose Quartz, Peridot
Libra	Opal, Diamond, Tourmaline, Malachite
Scorpio	Garnet, Rubellite, Agate, Imperial Topaz, Topaz, Obsidian, Bloodstone
Sagittarius	Amethyst, Blue Topaz, Hematite, Turquoise, Blue Zircon, Lapis Lazuli

Capricorn	Beryl, Onyx, Garnet
Aquarius	Blue Sapphire, Amethyst, Aquamarine
Pisces	Bloodstone, Jasper, Jade, Diamond, Aquamarine

SACRED SITES AND SACRED STONES

Stone worship is one of the earliest forms of religious and spiritual expression throughout the world. The great monoliths erected by ancient cultures were venerated because of their seeming agelessness and ability to resist the forces of decay and destruction which affect organic materials, including our own bodies. Used often as gateways to the sun, moon, and stars, the stones symbolized strength, unity, and the very dwelling place of the Gods.

Stones are symbols of permanence, representing the eternal and divine. They are linked to the Earth by their very nature—silicon, in the form of sand—which blends with water and becomes silicon dioxide, or quartz crystal. Stones are seemingly impervious to the elements, and are offspring of the Goddess' body, the Earth, embodying her sacred and mysterious qualities.

Probably the most famous of the sacred stones is the Lia Fail (La Fal), or "king stone" of Tara in Ireland, said to be one of the four sacred treasures of the ancient Gods, called the Tuatha De Dannan. Legend has it that when a rightful king touches this stone, it shrieks or cries out loudly. The Lia Fail stone was reputed to have veins of crystal running through it and was shaped like a pillar.

The Swearing Stone, or Cremave Stone, in Ireland was found in an ancient round temple by monks, who placed it in the monastery at Saints' Island. They used this stone, made of black marble flagstone, as a means for revealing the truth. A person suspected of a crime was brought to the stone, and if the accused lied, the stone placed a mark upon them and their family for seventeen generations. If no mark appeared, then the accused was deemed innocent. Legend proclaims that as long as the world exists, the Swearing Stone will retain its power.

The Stone of Destiny, also called the Stone of Scone, is a particularly famous king stone. Taken from the Scots by King Edward in 1296, this two hundred kilogram block of red sandstone has only recently been returned to Scotland. The Stone of Scone was brought to Scotland from Ireland, but legend claims that the stone came originally from Solomon's Temple. Some say the Stone of Scone and the Lia Fal are one and the same.

The Stone of Destiny is part of an ancient tradition which associates particular stones with the power of conferring kingship. According to this tradition, the king is divine or semi-divine, and a literal symbol of the land—i.e., the king and the land are one. This tradition was depicted in the legend of King Arthur, when he pulled the sword Excalibur from the stone.

Many globular ritual crystals have been found in Ireland. These probably were used in royal scepters or sacred shines. A very old crystal globe of this type was found at Currahmore. Most likely used for divination, the ball was of rock crystal, about the size of a large orange, encircled by a silver band.

Milky quartz, called "white stones" and "veins of the Great Mother Earth," have long been considered a link between our physical world and the divine otherworld. The ancient Irish people greatly valued the white stones and believed them to be pieces of the stars that had fallen to the Earth upon the arrival of the Gods. The building blocks for many of the prayer monuments found in Ireland were fashioned from the white stones. Throughout Great Britain, people still toss uncountable numbers of white pebbles and stones into ancient sacred wells and pools as offerings to the Goddess.

The druids considered the standing stones, such as Stonehenge, and the speaking stones (also called the "whisperers") to be alive. At Carnac in Brittany, three thousand stones are grouped in a five-mile area, and are a testament to the great effort required to build these stone edifices. Legends say supernatural star beings and giants erected these monoliths. There are stories of the stones moving and dancing on particular nights of power, or prophesying to passersby.

On the solstices and equinoxes, ancient peoples around the globe used light and shadow to align stones and stone structures with the sun and moon. These structures probably served as temples and as astronomical observatories. Before the Renaissance, no distinction existed between science and spirit, hence religious matters complemented and were interlaced with astronomy. For example, the Boyne Valley on the plains of Kildare in Ireland is the home of three megalithic mounds called Newgrange, Knowth, and Dowth, dating from between 3700 and 3200 B.C. The sacred stones at Newgrange are aligned to the position of the rising sun at the Winter Solstice. Legend says that the Tuatha De Dannan, the Divine Gods of Light, may have dwelt at Newgrange.

Sacred sites with sacred stones, often carved with symbols, are found in many parts of the world, including Europe, Egypt, Malta, Easter Island, Greece, the island of Crete, North America, Central America, Mexico, South America, the Pacific Islands, Asia, and Australia. Ceremonial events, planting, harvesting, and hunting times were based on the sun's position relative to the stones.

In Greek mythology the *omphalos*, the sacred stone of the Furies, was cone-shaped and one of the great sacred objects of the oracle at the Temple of Apollo at Delphi, together with the pit and the tripod. The *omphalos* represented the navel or center of the world. Zeus let loose two eagles at the ends of the Earth, and marked the spot where they met with a stone, the *omphalos*. This spot was guarded by two golden eagles. The *omphalos*, represented by navel- or cone-shaped stones, was worshipped throughout the Mediterranean. The Pythia of Apollo was empowered by the *omphalos*, who like Gaia, the Earth Goddess, uttered prophecies in a stone-cleft cave, guarded by a serpent.

In the legends of the Inca dynasty of South America, Manco Capac, first son of the sun, descended from the heavens to the valley of Cuzco in Peru. There he marked the center of the "Land of Four Quarters" by building the "Enclosure of Gold" known as the Temple of the Sun, which had a niche by the door that was covered in gold and gemstones. Regarded as a living incarnation of the sun, the emperor took a seat in this temple during solstice celebration ceremonies. The sun, reflecting off this niche of gold and gemstones, illuminated the chamber, bathing the emperor in golden light.

A Mayan ceremony still practiced today in the spring uses five stones which represent five magical positions of a cosmological pattern. The ritual reenacts creation, replicating the way the Gods fashioned the world at the beginning of time. The act of placing the stones in the northeast, northwest, southwest, southeast, and center also starts the new calendar by resetting the world in motion.

Contemporary Uses

PENDULUMS

Practiced by cultures throughout the world, divination is the ancient art of discovering the unknown or foretelling the future. There are many different tools and techniques for divination. The use of pendulums dates back as far as 10,000 years to the North American Eskimos, who used a walrus tooth attached to a cord. Archaeologists have uncovered dowsing pendulums dating back 5,000 years in mounds in Florida.

As a tool for receiving information from the higher self, the pendulum has evolved from its basic form of an animal tooth on a string to finely crafted items, made from various metals and stones. Crystals and gemstones in particular provide a very responsive medium, and are widely used as pendulums. Various types of quartz, such as clear, amethyst, rose, smoky, and citrine, make the most sensitive pendulums because they easily pick up changes and qualities of energy, including the energetic fields of our own bodies and the Earth, as well as those of the sun, moon, and stars.

You can buy a pendulum, readily available from New Age stores, pagan shops, and mail-order catalogs, or you can make your own. To make your own crystal or gemstone pendulum, take a small stone such as a pointed, clear quartz crystal and glue a bell cap on the end opposite the point. Tie a cord to it, six to twelve inches long, so the crystal dangles point down.

Pendulums help you tap into your subconscious mind, which records greater amounts of information from your senses than you are aware of on a conscious level. Also, pendulums help you connect into what Carl Jung termed the "cosmic unconscious" or "flow," also known as the Akashic Record, an etheric record of every action, thought, and detail of life on Earth.

When pendulum dowsing, the idea is not to obtain information that is 100 percent accurate all the time, but rather to use the pendulum as a way of gaining additional information, sometimes from unexpected sources, including elementals, devas, your inner self, and higher self, as well as spirit guides, extraterrestrials, and angels. Using a pendulum can enhance your decision-making process by helping you make more informed choices.

Following is the basic technique for pendulum dowsing. As you work with pendulums you will begin to get a feel for what works best for you, at which point you can expand or modify the technique. Always be sure to clear your pendulum stone before and after use.

1. Begin by having a clear image of what you want to know from the pendulum-dowsing process. This could take the form of a question, such as, "Should I take the new job that has been offered to me?" The question should be one that elicits a "yes" or "no" response.

2. Next, on a piece of paper draw a circle with a dot in the middle.

3. Grasp the string at the point where it connects to the stone. Move your thumb and forefinger gradually upward, allowing the pendulum to swing freely. At a certain point the stone will swing more strongly. Mark this anchor point with a knot. While holding the string at your anchor point, usually about four inches from the crystal, allow the crystal to dangle freely, with its point directly over the dot in the middle of circle.

4. Now, ask your higher self which point(s) on the circle mean "yes." If the crystal moves up and down, then mark the top and bottom of the circle "yes." Next, ask which point(s) are "no," and mark the answer accordingly. This establishes a baseline to work from. If you find you receive the same answer for "yes"

and "no," then clear your mind, and try asking again. One of the most important things in this process is to get your conscious mind out of the way, until you get a pure connection to the energetic source. Keep your hand steady while doing this procedure, allowing the pendulum to move on its own.

5. Once you have marked the circle, ask your question, and notice which way the pendulum moves relative to the markings on the circle. Again, if you have trouble getting an answer at first, clear your mind and try again.

Having mastered this basic technique, you can try more complex procedures, for instance, asking multiple choice questions by marking them on the circle. Marcel Vogel showed me a technique for locating lost objects or people, using a clear overlay marked with a grid and placed on top of a map or floor plan. Slowly move the pendulum over the grid until you receive a definite "yes" response. You can also experiment with tapping into and asking different sources for information, but remember to establish a baseline each time you use your pendulum, as this often changes day to day, or hour to hour.

Pendulums can be used to dowse energy fields in the Earth as well. Hold your pendulum in front of you, at arm's length, and begin walking slowly. Mentally direct the pendulum to begin moving when it detects an energy field. Move in and out of the field, noticing the response of the pendulum. After practicing this for a short time, you will become sensitized to the different densities and qualities of energetic fields. Your pendulum can be used to dowse for water in the same manner.

WANDS

Combining certain gemstones and metals with crystals in specific patterns creates a power wand that serves as a tool for amplifying, modifying, and focusing thought-forms and energy. The wand is an extension of the person using it, acting as an antenna. It receives, tunes, and transmits focused energy. Magical wands and wizard staffs are often made for specific purposes, such as second sight, divine knowledge, or dream enhancement. Likewise, the crowns and staffs of royalty were made by alchemists as powerful energy generators and shields.

A simple crystal wand can be made by inserting a single-terminated, clear quartz crystal into the end of a piece of copper tubing, or into the end of a wooden rod. To make a more complex wand, first decide what kind of material to use. Wood is traditional, but feel free to experiment and choose another medium, such as metal. When using wood for your wand, select a wood with which you have a special connection, one that embodies the qualities you desire for your spiritual work.

JEWELRY

Humankind has always had a craving for adornment. Often these adornments have symbolic importance or a practical function, showing the wearer's status or forming part of a person's religious trappings. Evidence has been found of the use of jewelry as long ago as the Paleolithic Age. Amulets are still worn in many parts of the world. Chosen for shape or color, or the importance of the place where they are found, stone amulets are considered to bestow protection and good luck. For example, in China children wear jade bracelets or anklets to protect them from harm.

When precious stones are made into jewelry or works of art, they become more precious. On a practical level, wearing a piece of quartz crystal jewelry helps balance your energetic field. Gemstones, when worn, emanate their individual qualities as well. To boost and balance your energy, the stone should make direct contact with your skin. Position your piece of crystal jewelry on the spot where you need energy most, or where you want to open up energy channels. For example, if you need personal empowerment, choose a pendant with a fire stone such as carnelian or rutilated quartz and wear it over your solar plexus. (Refer to page 79 for spiritual and healing properties of various gemstones.)

Pendants often combine the energies of several stones in the setting, and are most commonly worn over the thymus, or witness area. Amethyst has a calming effect when worn over the witness area, while tourmaline has a balancing or energizing effect. Wearing pendants thusly helps to balance emotions. In India, people traditionally wear certain combinations and arrangements of gemstones. Two examples are the "navaratna" (ruby, pearl, coral, emerald, topaz, diamond, sapphire, cat's eye, and amethyst), and the five-stone "pancharatna" (gold, amethyst, diamond, emerald, and pearl).

Wearing a crystal or gemstone pendant over the witness area stimulates the thymus gland, boosting your immune system and well-being. The heart chakra and the solar plexus are also very effective areas to wear crystal and gemstone pendants.

Rings are symbols of unity, eternity, rebirth, and natural cycles, and all rings were once sacred objects with protective powers. Originally, and once again today, with the advent of body piercing, rings are used to decorate fingers, ears, toes, tongues, noses, eyebrows, and belly buttons. Finger rings set with crystals and gemstones are often passed on from generation to generation. When buying a ring be certain it is compatible with you by first clearing it thoroughly, and then testing it by the simple kinesiology technique described in the chapter on choosing crystals and gemstones. Make sure the ring setting is open, so the stone touches your skin underneath.

Wearing rings on different fingers produces different effects because each finger impacts and corresponds to different parts of the body. The index, middle, and ring fingers are the most popular positions. Placing oils, essences, and herbs on the ring finger enhances their healing qualities in the body; rings with healing stones are best placed on the ring finger.

The tradition of ear piercing dates back to ancient times, when earrings were worn to protect the ears. Ear ornaments were part of the large number of amulets used to protect the openings of the body against dangerous spirits, powers, and morbid influences. Earrings serve to balance the left and right hemispheres of the brain, and also work on the acupressure points of the ear itself. If you choose to have your ears pierced, be aware of the specific points in the ear and how a hole in each spot will affect your body's energetic balance.

Bracelets and arm bands set with crystals and gemstones affect the side of the body you wear them on. Again, the setting should be open underneath to allow the stone to touch your skin. Worn on the left wrist or arm, the bracelet balances your spiritual or psychic energy. Worn on the right wrist or arm, bracelets strengthen your physical body and intellectual processes. Most wristwatches contain quartz crystals and affect the energy body. (Refer to page 79 for a list of the specific uses of stones when deciding which stones you want in a bracelet setting.)

Crystals can be worn with the point up or down. The point of the crystal directs the flow of energy. When pointed up in the setting, the stone will stimulate and energize the upper chakras, namely the throat, third eye, and crown. This position works well for meditation, channeling, or out-of-body experiences. When pointed down, the crystal has a grounding effect, and sometimes even a draining effect, because it moves your body's energy downward into the ground. The effect depends on whether the stone is capped with metal or cut on the top. A double terminated crystal is the best for daily wear, as it moves energy both up and down your chakras, amplifying the energy of your entire body.

All new jewelry should be cleared and cleaned before wearing. I suggest soaking your stones in sea salt and water for a few minutes. If you do not want to immerse the piece in water, place it in a bowl of sea salt and cover it for a few minutes. Jewelry worn on a daily basis often collects unwanted energy and needs to be cleared and reprogrammed every day. The pulsed breath technique is the easiest and most practical method for this.

Metals used in jewelry settings amplify the energetic effects of crystals and gemstones. Gold is the best metal because it strengthens your energy field, much as the sun vitalizes Earthly elements, but other metals also have healing and beneficial qualities. Following is a list of metal properties:

Metal	Properties
Copper	Setting sun energy, healing, excellent for conducting energy and for use in wands. Beware of any lead content in copper if used for jewelry.
Gold	Powerful sun energy. The higher the carat, the more powerful the energy. An excellent magnetic conductor for building personal life patterns, promoting growth and transcendence.

Platinum	Heavier than silver, and slightly magnetic. Multidimensional metal, good for out-of-body, shapeshifting, and multidimensional experiences.
Silver	Moon energy, emotional awareness, healing, balancing moon (water and tidal) energies, conducting feminine energy.
White Gold	Sun and moon energy combined together. Excellent for healing, conducting energy, balancing, and for personal empowerment.

FENG SHUI

Legend says the original Feng Shui masters learned their art from the Gods. Today this four thousand-year-old Eastern tradition is gaining widespread popularity, with several schools of Feng Shui in existence. Feng Shui means "the way of the wind and water," referring to the natural flow of energy in the universe. The basic concept of Feng Shui is to work in harmony with the elemental forces of the Earth and cosmos, rather than combating them, thus creating positive energy in your living and working environments.

Feng Shui practitioners know that all things are comprised of energy and emit energy fields. These fields can either enhance or harm your personal energy field. Energy enters the left side of your body and exits the right side, so carrying a crystal in your left pocket acts as a simple Feng Shui device by balancing your chi (Chinese word for "life energy"), especially if the crystal has been programmed with that intention.

Cutting fields, which are harmful configurations of energy, are called "sha." Feng Shui seeks to neutralize and transform cutting fields, or sha, into flowing chi by using various cures. A Feng Shui cure is a ritual, ceremony, technique, or item used in a certain way to repel or negate a cutting field of energy and/or to attract positive chi. You do not have to be a Feng Shui master or practitioner to use basic cures.

Crystals and gemstones are often used as cures because of their ability to disperse, pull, push, or scatter energy. When energy encounters a crystal ball, cluster, obelisk, or other shape, it slows down and diffuses in several directions, in much the same way light moves through a prism. The energy becomes fluid and can be molded and directed accordingly. One way to see the direction of the chi in a particular room or area is to smudge or light incense and watch the flow of smoke. The chi follows a similar pattern.

Faceted crystal balls transmute sha energy into chi energy. Crystal spheres or balls placed in windows send healing chi energy throughout the room. The ball captures the harsh sha energy, and the facets break up the sha into chi. This is the case with sha generated in a long hallway or corridor. In this application, notice whether the hallway or corridor is dark or lighted. Light, in tandem with crystals, is a particularly effective cure for transforming sha. Crystal chandeliers are used in this manner. A rule of thumb for hanging crystal chandeliers is for the fixture to be at least door height, 6 feet 8 inches, for the practical reason of not bumping your head on the fixture.

Keep a clear intent in mind when doing crystal placements, and always use your intuition and common sense when determining which size crystal to use for specific applications. Consider the scale within which you are working. For instance, a finger-sized crystal probably isn't sufficient for a large sliding glass window. A large cluster or well-placed sphere would be a much more effective cure.

Heavy objects, such as carved rock statues, large clusters, big stones, or generator crystals will absorb energy and/or force energy to move around them. Obelisks are especially powerful energy enhancers. Used in Feng Shui placement, they magnetize or pull energy into an area. Obelisks are made from many different types of stone, with quartz crystal obelisks being the most powerful, because their shape, in conjunction with their clarity, magnifies positive energy.

The color of crystals or stones is also important in Feng Shui. Using stones that complement the color scheme in a room creates a sense of harmony. Clear quartz is most commonly used because it reflects the spectrum of colors. Colored stones can also be used, with different colors providing various effects. Red is the color of vitality, and it attracts positive energy. Black also attracts energy, both positive and negative. Orange is the color of healing, gold the color of learning and mental activity, while green is the color of growth and creativity. Blue and white repel energy and can be used for protection from unwanted energies, while purple or indigo enhance spiritual and psychic harmony. In the workplace, a crystal paperweight, sphere, or cluster, placed on your desk or work table, is particularly effective for protecting you from any negative energy. In my experience, amethyst clusters are excellent when used in this capacity.

DREAMING

The way we live directly relates to the way we dream. Crystals and gemstones can enhance and clarify dream messages. Because dream stones are intimate and personal stones, you may not want other people to touch them.

One of the simplest methods for using stones in dreaming is to place the stone under your pillow before going to sleep. Clear and program the stone for specific dream qualities and/or particular dream messages. For example, Herkimer diamonds, kept in a pouch under your pillow or around your neck, are used to enhance dreaming. Amethyst used in dreaming pulls in spiritual energies and enhances your intuitive abilities. I prefer moonstone, clear quartz, malachite, bloodstone, azurite, and fluorite for dreaming purposes. To stop nightmares try citrine, obsidian, ruby, carnelian, and clear quartz. To enhance creative ideas and thoughts in dreams, use bloodstone at your feet. (For additional information on stone qualities and uses, refer to page 79.)

Another easy way to use dream stones is to place one or two stones next to your bed, on a bedside table or bookcase. Pointing a single-terminated clear quartz crystal toward your body will have the effect of bringing energies into your energetic sphere. Pointing the tip away from your body will facilitate out-of-body experiences while dreaming.

You can place a grid around your bed using clear quartz crystals. Start with one stone at the head of the bed, pointing it inward or outward, depending on your preference and intention. Dream with that stone for a week, then add another clear point at your feet. Again, dream with the stone for one week. Add two more stones, one at a time, on each side of your bed, waiting one week between placement. Another method of grid placement for balance is to place the stones on the north, south, east, and west directional points around your bed, in that order. If at any time, one of the stones is not harmonious to your sleep and dreaming, select another stone. If you sleep with someone else, the stones will also affect them.

To clarify and enhance dream messages and content, use three cleaned and programmed quartz crystals. Lie on your back and place one crystal on your third eye (forehead), and one in each hand. For about five minutes, visualize or sense yourself being filled with white light coming from the stones. Breathe the light in from the crystals, and then focus on a particular person or event that you want to dream about. Ask yourself a main question about the matter, repeating it over and over to yourself, either silently or aloud. Allow yourself to drift to sleep. When you awaken, lie completely still for a few minutes, rub the crystals in your hands and try to recall your dreams. Be sure to record or write down what you recall.

One of my favorite dream techniques using stones is a shapeshifting process. Malachite, geodes, clear quartz, azurite, aventurine, emerald, ruby, and lapis lazuli are excellent stones for this purpose. A favorite stone you have found in nature also works well. Begin by closing your eyes and breathing deeply, relaxing as much as possible. Sense yourself sinking into the stone, starting with your toes and moving up your body. Feel your flesh and bones sinking completely into the lattice of the stone. Meld with the stone and become one with it. Now, in your mind's eye, sense the animal or object of your choice. Choose something simple at first, like a sphere of colored energy. Look at the sphere of energy from every angle, and move around it in your mind's eye. Melt into the sphere, into the other, and become one with it. Allow yourself to drift into sleep in this shapeshifted form. When you awaken, rub the stone in your hands, and write down or record whatever you can recall about your dream.

Dreaming can also be used for healing. Rutilated quartz is particularly good for this purpose because it accelerates tissue regeneration. Place a rutilated quartz crystal in your left hand and make an effort to go to the source of your illness or pain. See or sense yourself as completely healthy and full of energy. Imagine moving this image into the stone. Sense the image being transferred from the stone into your body with each breath you take. Give yourself the suggestion to release the old, unwanted dream of illness you have been carrying with you and replace it with a dream of total well-being, harmony, and happiness. Breathe deeply, and allow yourself to drift to sleep. Repeat this process twenty-one times consecutively.

Healing Uses

CRYSTAL HEALING

As the growing field of psychoneuroimmunology indicates, our state of mind has a great influence on our state of health. The physical, mental, spiritual, and energetic go hand in hand. Energetic disturbances or blockages occur whenever there is injury, illness, or trauma in your life. During the healing process, you remove these blockages, restoring a healthy energy pattern to that part of your body. Every injury and emotional hurt takes a little bit of light out of your energy field. Crystal healing restores that light, renews the energy, and gives you an opportunity to be healthy again.

Through pain, your body receives the signal to pay attention. Dis-ease or illness begins on an energetic level before being transferred into the mental and physical levels. Pain is a by-product of energy blockages. One extremely effective method of removing these blockages is by using crystals.

Crystal healing, based on the transfer of energy from the crystal into the body, and vice versa, is an extremely effective method of removing these blockages. Crystals are silicates, which constitute the largest and most common class of minerals found throughout the world. Quartz crystals contain silicon and oxygen, a combination found in most minerals on our planet. Our bodies also contain silicon dioxide, suggesting a genuine physical connection with crystals. In addition to silicon and oxygen, water is often present in many type of quartz crystals. The human body is made up mostly of water.

The atomic similarities between crystals and the human body allow for the communication and transfer of energy, often benefiting our well-being. For example, carrying a crystal in your pocket or wearing one in a pendant that is cleared and programmed on a regular basis increases the strength of your energy field. This in turn shields you from negative thoughts and emotions emanating from other people. Your intention directs the energetic activity of the crystal. Crystal healing is effective on its own, or you can combine it with other healing methods, such as nutrition therapy, therapeutic massage, visualization, and hypnosis.

Utilizing color and light enhances crystal healing. Begin practicing with colors by gathering colored objects like small panes of glass, pieces of fabric, or paper. Focus on the color and practice pulsing the hue into the stone to charge it with a specific color essence. The following is a list of colors with their corresponding healing properties:

Blue: Used when you begin a healing work, blue cleans out any negativity. Imagine a brilliant electric blue or cobalt blue light or wave of energy washing out your stone and your energy field.

Green: After flushing the energy out with blue, green sets up new healthy patterns in the energetic field. See or sense forest green or bright kelly green, the color of health, abundance, and nature, and pulse this color into your stone and into your entire being.

Gold: Gold fuels the new healthy pattern. Visualize and/or sense the gold of the sun warming and energizing the new healthy pattern. Pulse this hue into the stone and your energy field.

White: This color is used for awareness of your higher self and spiritual path.

Rose: For a sense of love, use rose, especially when dealing with emotional issues in the healing.

Remember, you are a catalyst or channel for energy in the healing process. When doing healing work, the more you can step aside and move out of your ego the better the results.

GEMSTONE ESSENCES

As an alternative vibratory aid, gemstone essences help balance your body and energy. You can purchase them or make them yourself at home. Sometimes the stone is ground into a powder and then mixed into a tincture, but this is not necessary in order to access the healing qualities within the stone.

Make crystal and gemstone essences or tinctures by placing a crystal or gemstone in a glass of water for several hours. After you remove the stone the liquid will be imbued with its essential properties. The elixir can be drunk or applied topically. You can place a few drops of the essence on a piece of personal jewelry, or on a crystal for healing or enhancing meditation. When you wear the jewelry or use the crystal, the gemstone essence is transferred into your body, and will remain until the essence is washed off or cleared from the stone.

Marcel Vogel used quartz crystals to charge or "structure" water and other liquids such as wine and fruit juice. You can try this yourself by first clearing and programming a quartz crystal. An appropriate program would be to fill the crystal with energy, light, and love. After programming, place the crystal in the liquid for at least two hours. Drink the beverage and notice the difference in taste. The liquid generally tastes smoother and has a noticeable sweetness.

Gemstone Essence Recipes:

Aquamarine Essence: For a gently cleansing gemstone essence, place a cleared and programmed aquamarine stone in a glass of spring water. Let the glass sit outside in the moonlight for at least three hours. Remove the stone from the liquid and drink it.

Amethyst Essence: Use a stone that has not been set, placing it in a small, clear glass bottle. Mix two parts spring or distilled water to one part grain alcohol. Cover and set in direct sunlight for at least six hours. Use a few drops at a time to deepen meditation, enhance your receptivity to spirit, and as a remedy for internal parasites.

Emerald Essence: Use two parts distilled or spring water with one part 180-proof grain alcohol, and add a well-colored, uncut emerald crystal that has not been placed in a setting. For four ounces of liquid, use at least one carat of rough stone, to a maximum of four carats. Bring the mixture to a gentle boil in a Pyrex pan or glass coffee pot, then cover and simmer for thirty minutes. When the mixture cools, put it in a clear glass bottle with a stopper and place it in direct sunlight for at least six hours. Store the tincture in a green glass bottle. Use two to nine drops of tincture in a glass of water or wine. Used for balancing body, mind, and spirit, emerald essence is especially healing for heart, spleen, and sacral centers, and acts as an internal stabilizer and tranquilizer.

SELF-HEALING TECHNIQUES

You can use crystal healing techniques on yourself as well as other people. Following are four techniques for self-healing:

Technique #1: Hold your crystal in your left (receiving) hand and close your eyes. Visualize a brilliant white light emanating from the crystal into your hand, up your arm, and into your entire body. See the light fill and surround your body, until it seems as though you are wrapped in a cocoon of white light. Breathe in the light. Small, clear, and rutilated quartz balls are excellent for this technique. Be sure to clear your crystal when finished.

Technique #2: Hold your crystal over your solar plexus, pointing up. Visualize or sense a ball of golden energy coming from the crystal into your solar plexus area. Feel the golden light warm the area, and then with your breath, expand the light outward into your head and limbs. Expand the light outward about an arm's length distance from your body, surrounding yourself with warm, golden light. Bathe in the light for about ten minutes. Clear your stone when you are finished.

Technique #3: Breathe while asking yourself about any sensations and impressions in the problem area. Try to sense the color and texture of the area, and if there are any feelings, sounds, or images contained there. Place the crystal on your body, and fill it with your awareness of the illness or pain. Do this as many times as it takes to remove all of the pain or illness. Clear the stone when you are done.

Technique #4 (Seven-Step Vogel Self-Healing Technique):

1. Hold your healing crystal with both hands in front of you. In your mind's eye, go to the problem area.
2. Make an effort to find the root cause of the problem. Breathe deeply and rhythmically, and focus on as many details of the problem as you can.
3. Release the problem and cause, using the pulsed breath technique. With your mind, transfer the problem or blockage into the crystal.
4. Visualize the healed area alive, flowing with energy, and whole.
5. Fill the area with white light and thoughts of love, harmony, and well-being.
6. Clear and clean the crystal.
7. Repeat the procedure three times.

TREATING COMMON AILMENTS

The solar plexus and the heart region are the two major energy centers in the body. The solar plexus acts as a window to the past, and the heart region is a window to the present and future. Use any of the following techniques to move the energy up through the solar plexus and through the heart area, continuing upward through the chakras (see chart, page 63). You can also work along meridian lines and acupressure points with the crystal. The most effective healing distance is 1 to 1 1/2 inches above the skin.

Headaches: For headaches, place a pain reliever, such as white willow, on your healing crystal. Place the crystal on your forehead and draw your breath in and pulse your breath out. The essence of the pain reliever will be absorbed by your etheric body, and you will feel relief.

Another method is to place the healing crystal (citrine is the best for headaches) directly on your forehead, back of the neck, temples, or wherever the pain is located. Breathe the pain into the crystal, and then clear the crystal using the pulsed breath technique, salt, or smudging. Repeat three times or until the pain subsides.

Muscular Pain (Including Lower Back Pain): Many of us experience lower back pain because of the frustration of not being supported or the inability to achieve what we desire. Because most people spend several hours a day sitting down, this frustration locks in and becomes focused in the solar plexus. Stress and anger fuel the problem by causing blockage in the solar plexus which prevents emotions from flowing.

Working with another person, use the seven-step Vogel Healing Technique, focusing on the area between the base of the spine and the skull. Rotating the crystal clockwise, draw in your breath, and release the locked energy along the spine. Repeat this procedure three times. When working locally, place your hand directly behind the problem area.

Injuries and Wounds: If you have just suffered an injury, position your healing crystal, with its tip pointing toward your head, on the area of injury. Leaving the crystal in place for a few minutes will generally reduce pain and swelling of the tissues. As it absorbs the pain and imbalance of the injury, clear it with the pulsed breath technique and reprogram it repeatedly, until the pain, bleeding, swelling, and redness subside.

CHAKRA BALANCING AND LAYOUTS

To balance your chakras using a clear quartz crystal, first clear and clean your crystal. Then program it for balance. Hold the crystal over each of your seven chakras (at the crown, third eye, throat, heart, solar plexus, just above your navel, and sacral areas) checking for blockages of energy. The chakra area should vibrate and feel warm when working with crystals and stones. If it feels lifeless, pulse your breath through the crystal with the intention of opening the chakra area. Use the mental command "Open." Do this process slowly, and remember you are dealing with very real energies, even if they are subtle. Balancing your chakras helps restore health and clear the mind.

Stone Color, Chakra, and Sound Relationships

Stone Color	Chakra	Sound (Note)
Red	First	C
Red-Orange, Orange	Second	D
Yellow-Orange, Yellow/Gold	Third	E
Yellow-Green, Green	Fourth	F
Blue-Green, Sky Blue	Fifth	G
Dark Blue, Indigo/Violet	Sixth	A
White/Clear	Seventh	B

Chakra Layouts

The following layouts provide a framework; feel free to adapt them according to your own intuition. Clear and program each of the stones before using it, and clean and clear the stones after you are finished. To determine which stones work best on specific areas, my suggestion is to try at least two different types of stone on each chakra. Stone types and placements will vary, depending on the person.

Healing Layout

The purpose of this layout is to facilitate healing, first on an energetic level, which then carries over to the physical. Two stones for each chakra position are suggested. Try one stone, and then the other, testing which one works best for you. Place your cleared and programmed stones in a basket or on a cloth next to you. Laying comfortably on your back, begin placing the stones on your body, from the lower chakras up to the crown. Breathe deeply and visualize or sense a bright golden or white, warm and healing light radiating from the stones and filling your body. Allow the stones to remain in position for at least fifteen minutes, and then remove them, one by one, in the reverse order you placed them on your body, from the crown down to the base.

Crown (Top of head)—Clear Quartz or Rutilated Quartz

Third Eye (Between and above eyebrows)—Amethyst or Moonstone

Throat (Center of base of neck)—Sodalite or Lapis Lazuli

Heart (Center of chest)—Rose Quartz or Jade

Solar Plexus (Below breastbone)—Gold Calcite or Carnelian

Navel Chakra (Just below navel)—Red Jasper or Bloodstone

Root or Base Chakra (Between genitals and anus)—Onyx or Hematite

Meditation Layout

The purpose of this layout is to enhance personal meditation and communication with the divine. Again, there are two suggested stones for each chakra. Lay the stones out beginning with the root or base chakra, and finishing at the crown. Breathe deeply and meditate as usual. Allow the stones to remain in position for at least half an hour, up to eight hours,

Healing Layout

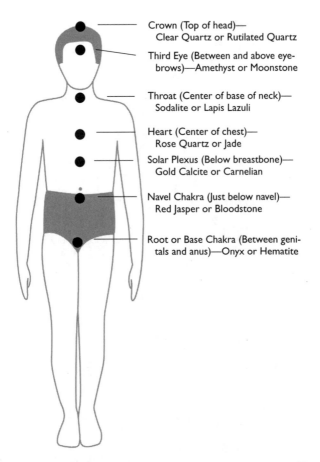

Crown (Top of head)—
Clear Quartz or Rutilated Quartz

Third Eye (Between and above eyebrows)—Amethyst or Moonstone

Throat (Center of base of neck)—
Sodalite or Lapis Lazuli

Heart (Center of chest)—
Rose Quartz or Jade

Solar Plexus (Below breastbone)—
Gold Calcite or Carnelian

Navel Chakra (Just below navel)—
Red Jasper or Bloodstone

Root or Base Chakra (Between genitals and anus)—Onyx or Hematite

Meditation Layout

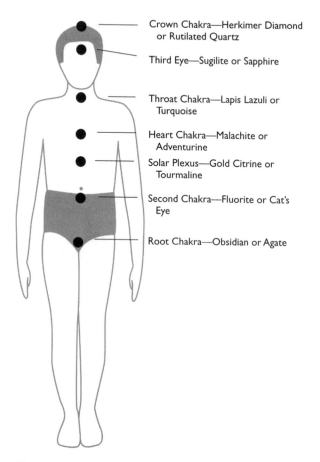

Crown Chakra—Herkimer Diamond or Rutilated Quartz

Third Eye—Sugilite or Sapphire

Throat Chakra—Lapis Lazuli or Turquoise

Heart Chakra—Malachite or Adventurine

Solar Plexus—Gold Citrine or Tourmaline

Second Chakra—Fluorite or Cat's Eye

Root Chakra—Obsidian or Agate

leaving the stones on your body while you sleep if you desire. Remove the stones in reverse order.

Crown Chakra (Top of head)—Herkimer Diamond
Third Eye (Between and above eyebrows)—Sugilite or Sapphire
Throat (Center of base of neck)—Lapis Lazuli or Turquoise
Heart (Center of chest)—Malachite or Aventurine
Solar Plexus (Below breastbone)—Gold Citrine or Tourmaline
Sacral Areas (Below navel)—Fluorite or Cat's Eye
Root or Base Chakra (Between genitals and anus)—Obsidian or Agate

MARCEL VOGEL HEALING TECHNIQUE

Originated by Dr. Marcel Vogel, my friend and teacher, this remains the most effective healing technique I have seen demonstrated or personally experienced. When working with another person the primary intention is to help your partner bring her body into balance, so her energy field flows in a healthy, natural pattern. Your role is to act as a conduit for healing energy.

The Eight Healing Motions

The healing crystal is always held with the operating tip pointing out and up. In this position the crystal generates a field of energy that oscillates with the energy field surrounding the body.

Most people prefer to hold the healing crystal in the right (sending) hand, but this is not an absolute rule. Try both hands and see which one works best.

Finger positions and hand motions influence and enhance the effectiveness of your crystals. Generally, position either your index or middle finger on one of the crystal tip faces. This regulates the intensity of the energy field emanating from the tip of the crystal. As you move your finger closer to the tip, the field becomes narrower, and as you slide your finger down toward the base of the crystal, the field becomes broader.

Your thumb acts as a sensor, and with it, you can vary the vibrational rate of the crystal and the frequency of oscillation released through the crystal, by moving your thumb up and down the surface of the crystal.

Four basic hand motions are used with crystals: a clockwise, circular motion that moves energy into the treatment area; a counterclockwise, circular motion that pulls energy out of the treatment area or withdraws the charge; a steady motion, with slight movements, while finding the optimum position for greatest field strength; and an up and down motion, and back and forth (stitching) motion which creates an oscillating field vibration.

When you are working in a circular motion, you are visualizing light, and when working with the crystal in an up and down motion, the focus is on vibration and sound.

The energy emanating from a charged crystal forms a spiral. When you rotate the crystal, the spiral flows outward and becomes stronger with each spin, building up a greater linkage between you and the focus of your crystal.

Healing Dialogue

Establishing rapport and trust by communicating with your partner plays an integral part in any healing. Start by asking the key question, "Do you want to be healed?" Although this may seem obvious, sometimes a person doesn't really want to resolve a problem, be it spiritual, emotional, or physical. Everyone deals with personal issues at their own pace, so be sure you receive an affirmative response. If you receive a negative or fearful response in any form, whether verbal, physical, or psychic, it is not wise to continue the healing.

Preparing for a Healing

After receiving the affirmation from your partner, the next step involves merging with divine energy. Whatever your preference—the Spirit, Divine Mind, Oneness, or Cosmic Consciousness—link yourself with this energy to facilitate the highest possible benefit from the healing. Now is the time for prayer and asking for divine guidance and help in the healing.

Ask your partner to remove all jewelry, belts, and coins from her pockets, and any metal objects from her body. Your partner should avoid wearing clothes with metal buttons, zippers, or hooks during the healing, as the metal creates a "false" energetic field in those areas. Be sure to clear all jewelry before putting it back on at the conclusion of the healing session.

Provide a stool or chair for your partner to sit on, one which gives you access to both the front and back of her body. Because this healing method is very powerful, she may go limp during the process, making it essential that she be supported in some way.

Build a state of equilibrium by creating an envelope of energy around yourself, which looks like a cocoon of white light, edged in cobalt blue. This serves as a form of protection, especially important when working in stressful situations. While you are building this field of energy around you, send thoughts of harmony, love, balance, and inner strength to your partner. This will increase your partner's energy field prior to the healing work, and prevent you from being drained during the procedure.

Crystal Healing Process

Begin by handing your partner the healing crystal. Ask her to breathe her energy into it. This creates a union between you and your partner, within the crystal. Also, the more actively your partner participates in the healing, the better the results will be. While your partner merges with the healing crystal, continue gently questioning her regarding the problem, and how long it has lasted. Next ask whether she is ready to release the problem and let go of the root cause of the imbalance. Give praise and encouragement if you receive a positive reply.

Now take your healing crystal back and slowly scan your partner's etheric field by holding the crystal in your right hand, tip pointed toward her and slightly upward. Place your left hand on her back, opposite the crystal. Your left hand serves as an anchor. If you prefer, you can work with your hand and the crystal about an inch away from the surface of the body. Scan the body with your crystal, using small circular motions, combined with slow, up and down motions, to gather energetic information. Notice any sensations you experience or sudden energetic messages.

Breathing with your partner, use your breath to obtain a clearer indication of the energetic flows and streams of her body by breathing deeply and rhythmically. Continue to move your left hand in unison with your right hand, like a shadow. Move the crystal along the chakra line, and notice any areas that seem hot or cold, dark or gray. These are generally places of energetic imbalance. Be sure to ask your partner what, if any, trauma occurred in these areas, or if she is having discomfort or pain in these particular places.

After scanning the body, move your healing crystal over the thymus, or witness, area, 3 to 5 inches below the throat chakra. Take a deep breath and hold it, and at the same time use a counterclockwise twist of the crystal, and then rotate it slightly, to enter your partner's subtle energy body. Resume breathing, remembering to synchronize your breathing with your partner. You and your partner may feel a tugging sensation when you connect with the etheric body. This is completely normal. Use diagonal and horizontal stitching motions with the crystal, and then move on to small clockwise circular motions over the body's surface. The stitching motions tie the energy field together and can be used all over the energy body.

Next, hold the crystal on the problem area and have your partner see and sense the problem as clearly as possible. Increase in speed the small circular motions with the crystal. Ask her to draw in a deep breath with you and hold it: give the voice command to release the problem. Release your breath together with force by pulsing it through your nose. Your healing crystal is at its optimum effectiveness when you draw your breath in and hold it. By holding your breath, you build and strengthen the charge to its maximum potential.

Shake off the build-up of unwanted energy from your healing crystal using a snap of your wrist while pulsing your breath. While doing this, visualize a clear, cobalt blue light washing through your crystal. Go back to the same area and repeat the "release" process two times.

Next, use clockwise circular motions to fill the area with energy and light, moving through the colors blue, green, and gold in succession. Finish by using large, circular and up and down sweeping motions with both of your hands holding the crystal, 4 to 6 inches from the surface of the skin. Visualize her body being filled with bright, white light, and direct your positive and loving thoughts her way. This builds a new, healthy pattern of energy in your partner's etheric body.

Exit the etheric body at the same place you entered (the witness area) with a small, clockwise twist of your wrist. Stand your partner up slowly and give her a big hug. Marcel Vogel always emphasized ending each crystal healing with a warm, compassionate hug. Have your partner drink six to eight glasses of water each day for the next two days as a way to flush out the toxins released during the healing session. Be sure to clear your crystal after the healing, and before putting it away.

Grids, Gazing, and Ritual

CRYSTAL GRIDS

Crystals and gemstones, positioned in specific geometric patterns, produce unified energy fields called grid systems. Grid systems manifest a certain energy vortex that results in higher octaves of energy and light becoming more pronounced within them. In this way, a grid acts as the meeting ground between this planet and other energetic dimensions, opening a communication link for accessing healing energies, information, and knowledge from the many realms of existence.

Every time you form a grid, you create an energy mandala or light pattern that facilitates a healing and spiritual experience. Placing the grid stones in harmonious positions is imperative. When you point two or more of the grid stones at a specific area, this focuses healing energy on that area. Pointing stones inward adds healing energy to the grid, while pointing stones outward disperses the negative energy from inside the grid. Rely on your common sense, intuition, spiritual guidance, and experience when deciding how to position and use stones.

Each kind of crystal and gemstone has its own healing and spiritual uses as listed in the following chapter. When you begin placing stones together in grids, the energies of the stones blend, producing a synergistic effect. When creating a crystal grid, clear quartz is often preferable because it is easier to program than other crystals, but using different kinds of stones produces an unlimited number of patterns and healing effects. The choice depends on your intentions and needs.

Clear and program each crystal or gemstone. Having a specific intention when you program a grid serves to strengthen the energy mandala and vortex. You can also use breath, music, drumming, chanting, color, scent, and textures to amplify the grid energy and effect. Another way to enhance the energy is by holding crystals or stones of similar types and sizes in your hands while laying or sitting in a grid.

Often a grid contains a focal crystal, which is usually the crystal placed at your head or feet. Using your breath, begin at this focal point, and visualize or sense an energetic silver or gold thread connecting the grid stones in a clockwise circle. Do this three times to strengthen the grid field. When you are finished with the grid, pull up the grid stones in the reverse order in which you laid them down, and be sure to clean and clear your stones before putting them away.

When you use clusters in grids, the energy mandala will take on a more complex pattern. Be aware of this when positioning and connecting your clusters. You can use pyramids, obelisks, and other cut shapes in grids, but remember, like clusters, they add more dimensions to the field or energy mandala.

Multi-purpose Healing Grid: Eight clear quartz crystals placed around you in an oval; two each at your shoulders, hips, knees (psychic entry points), one positioned at your head and one at your feet, as shown in the layout. Infuse the crystals with healing color, visualizing and/or sensing blue, green, gold, and then white light radiating from the stones. Mentally connect the crystals with a gold or silver thread of light in a clockwise pattern, starting at the focal crystal, which is the crystal placed at your head. Use your breath to move the energy and light through the crystals.

Multi-purpose Layout
(supine position)

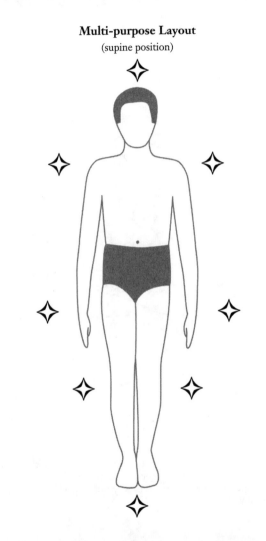

Body Mind Layout

Grid for Body, Mind, and Spirit Balance: Three crystals. Connect the stones with a silver or gold energetic thread in a pyramid shape, starting with the focal crystal, which is the crystal in front of you.

Meditation Layout

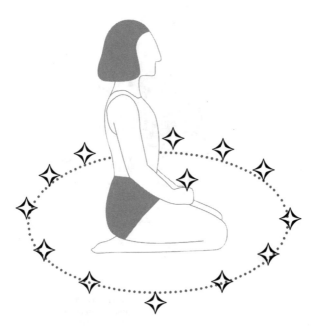

Meditation Grid: Twelve crystals, plus focal crystal (thirteen total), placed in a circle as shown. Hold your focal crystal in your hands, and connect the stones in a clockwise pattern, starting at the focal crystal.

Elements Layout

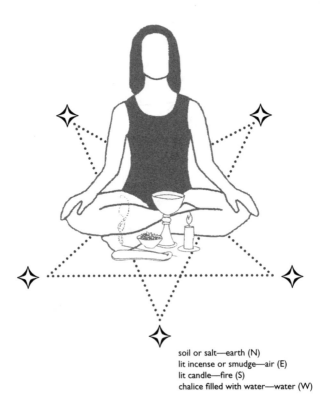

soil or salt—earth (N)
lit incense or smudge—air (E)
lit candle—fire (S)
chalice filled with water—water (W)

Grid for Communicating with the Elements: Five crystals in pentagram configuration. Place yourself and the elements (earth, air, fire, and water) in the center of the grid.

Ancestral Layout

(placed behind you)

Ancestral Contact: Nine crystals, placed in a Tree of Life configuration. Connect the stones in a clockwise pattern starting at the roots of the tree. Use an heirloom or something dating from the approximate time period you wish to enter, for instance, a picture or coin.

CRYSTAL GAZING

Crystal gazing differs from scrying in that the intention of gazing is to imprint the crystal with particular sensual or energetic instructions, as opposed to staring into the crystal for divination purposes. What causes the crystal to become imprinted is your intention and desire. This was a concept Marcel Vogel often repeated to me. You begin to charge the crystal just by looking at it, even for a moment. By using your breath in conjunction with your intention, you increase and maximize the charge transfer.

Clear quartz crystal is the most commonly used stone for gazing, but tourmaline, ruby, beryl, citrine, moonstone, garnet, and amethyst are also excellent choices, depending on the desired result. When done properly, the crystal gazing process is a powerful tool for self-transformation and actualizing your dreams.

A basic technique involves gazing into the crystal and imagining yourself moving into the stone. From inside the crystal, begin to see the room you are in: the details of the walls and furnishings, the floor, ceiling, and finally yourself.

The following are two specific crystal gazing processes. Using these as a basis, be creative with your uses of crystal gazing.

Technique #1—Crystal Gazing for Prosperity and Abundance
Think of your favorite shade of green, preferably a kelly, forest, or grass green. Find something that color—paper, a plant, clothing, food—and place it in front of you. Focus your attention on the color for a few moments. Using a clear quartz crystal that has been physically cleaned and energetically cleared, hold the stone cradled in your hands, while pulsing the hue into the stone with your breath. Gaze at the stone from every angle while turning it over in your hands. To enhance the process, you can create a backlight for the stone by using candles, a flashlight, or

small lamp. Sense the color green moving into each face of the crystal and into the very lattice structure and atoms that make up the stone. See, feel, taste, smell, hear, and intuit the color green moving deep into the crystal. Gaze at the stone for about ten minutes or until your eyes start watering. Repeat this procedure three times, building the vibrancy of the color with each repetition. Carry the "green" crystal with you or place it in a prominent position such as your desk, or wherever you want to bring abundance and prosperity into your life. Be careful not to put the crystal directly on your computer, as the energetic fields of stones sometimes adversely affect electronic equipment.

Technique #2—Crystal Gazing for Creativity

Select a specific creative project such as a book, work of art, song, garden, interior design, and so forth. Be certain this is something you really want to create. On a piece of paper write down as many details as possible and your goal(s) regarding the project. For example, if you select writing a book, describe the cover, the spine with the title and your name, the jacket, and the interior text, as well as how many copies will be printed, marketing strategies, speaking engagements, etc. Use a cleared and cleaned clear quartz crystal for the gazing process. With both hands, hold the stone in front of you at eye level, and begin to visualize the book and all of these details entering into the crystal and becoming implanted into its internal lattice and atoms. Pulse these images into the crystal with your breath to strengthen the charge. See and sense yourself after the completion of the creative project. Gaze steadily at the crystal for about ten minutes, holding it alternately in your right and left hand, all the while imprinting it with images and sensations related to the desired results for the project. Repeat this process three times. Carry, wear, or place the crystal in a prominent position until the project comes to fruition. Upon success, clear the stone out.

RITUAL AND CEREMONY

Traditionally, shamans conducted ceremonies and made offerings on natural altars and in sacred groves. These were places where the presence of divinities was most felt; at the sources of water, in the depths of sacred caves, in underground repositories, and in the basins where the steps led down to the underworld.

Stones are connected to the element of earth, representative of the north direction. In ceremony and ritual, the north point is considered the home of knowledge and divine wisdom. Earth symbolizes the physical universe, with its concrete goals and objectives.

Crystals and gemstones, used as ritual and ceremonial gifts, figure prominently in wiccanings, initiations, handfastings, and funerals. For example, infants are given special stones to protect, guide, and strengthen them upon birth. Initiation necklaces, rings, or bracelets are traditionally made of metal, crystal, and gemstones, and given to new initiates. Wives and husbands exchange crystals and gemstones as tokens of their loving intentions during handfasting ceremonies. Rings, other jewelry, and ceremonial stones are often buried with the dead to protect them and guide them into the otherworld.

Clear quartz crystals, with fine points, make excellent Watchtower Crystals, used to mark the four corners of your sacred ritual circle. Select four crystals to represent the elemental qualities: earth for the north point; air for the east point; fire for the south point; and water for the west point. A fifth central crystal is optional and represents spirit. Program these crystals with the energy of their respective points. Each time you create or draw a sacred ceremonial circle, use these crystals to mark the four corners and center. Leave the stones in place during the complete ritual, pulling them up at the same time you pull up your sacred circle. Do not clear or reprogram these crystals.

For the following ritual, you will need a picture that represents your goal, a crystal or gemstone, a quiet location, and a positive intention. Meditate with the stone and the picture, and carry them both with you for at least a week before doing the ritual. Through this process, the stone becomes attuned to the image and to your vibration. Work with the stone and picture three times a day, morning, noon, and evening, putting a small amount of an appropriate essential oil on the stone each time you handle it. Communicate with the stone, telling it the purpose of the ritual and what you want it to do for you. Use your breath to pulse the image, as well as your thoughts and feelings surrounding the ritual, into the stone. Take the stone and picture out, place them on your altar or sacred space, and use them as focal points during your ritual. If you are performing a ritual to rid yourself of unwanted energy or relationships, bury the stone and picture after the ritual in a deep, safe, undisturbed spot. Do not reuse or unearth the stone.

Small bits of crystal and gemstone can be placed in vials of ritual oil to consecrate the oil. First clear and program the tiny stones carefully, then hold the stones and the vial of oil in your hands and connect with your version of the Divine, with the intention of consecrating the stones and oil. Then put the stones into the vial. Make sure the stone is harmonious with the oil you place it in. For example, small amethyst crystals are excellent when placed in honeysuckle oil. Small citrine crystals combine well with rosemary oil. Consecrated oils have a long shelf life and can be kept and used for a long time.

Healing and Spiritual Properties of Crystals and Gemstones

LIST OF STONES

Agate, Blood Agate, Red Agate, Banded Agate, Moss Agate, Blue Lace Agate, Brown Agate, White Agate, Black Agate, Green Agate

Color: Variegated and banded, translucent and sometimes transparent, white to gray, brown, blue, black.

Healing and Spiritual Uses: A kind of chalcedony comprised of microscopic quartz crystals, agate is excellent for emotional and physical balancing, digestion, grounding, building healthy energy patterns and self-confidence, longevity, protection, self-honesty, scrying, reducing stress, and blood circulation.

Amazonite, Amazonstone (Feldspar)

Color: Blue-green, green.

Healing and Spiritual Uses: Finding personal truth, luck, prosperity, successful completion, growth, soothing energy, creativity, psychic ability, and receiving energy.

Amethyst

Color: Light to dark purple, dark purple-red, deep violet to pale lavender to almost clear.

Healing and Spiritual Uses: Spiritual development, divine connection, mental clarity, healing, balancing and controlling temperament, love, divination, wisdom, courage, psychic growth, dreaming, protection, and invulnerability. Curbs the urge to drink alcohol, helps to overcome addiction, and increases hormone production. Beneficial for the circulatory and nervous system, relaxation, astral travel, doubling out, which is being in the physical world and in an "other" world at the same time; seeing beyond illusions, and banishing nightmares.

Aquamarine

Color: Green, pale blue-green, aqua.

Healing and Spiritual Uses: Form of beryl utilized for clarity of perception and eyesight, releasing old patterns and conditioning, flow of creativity, inspiration, peace of mind, multidimensional experience, protection, courage, centering, purification and cleansing, calming and soothing energy, reducing fears, and sharpening intuition.

Aventurine

Color: Green, red, blue, brown.

Healing and Spiritual Uses: Positive participation, growth, healing, general well-being, activating the imagination, creativity, prosperity, good luck charm, and travel amulet. Strengthens eyesight, increases perception, and calms emotions.

Azurite

Color: Blue, blue-green (with Malachite), copper flecks.

Healing and Spiritual Uses: Copper-based, called the "jewel of wisdom," azurite is beneficial for amplifying healing ability and energy, gaining insight, mental clarity and control, enhancing meditation, and prenatal strength.

Benitoite

Color: Pink, white, purple, blue, or translucent.

Healing and Spiritual Uses: Benefits the pituitary gland, improves intuition, communication with the Earth, growing patterns, and gardening.

Beryl, Heliodor

Color: Yellow, white, blue, gold, green, blue-green.

Healing and Spiritual Uses: Relieves stress and provides clarity. Helpful for discarding unwanted memories and habits.

Strengthens circulation, boosts the immune system, clears eyesight. Enhances verbal communication and expression, reawakens love, romance, and self-responsibility.

Black Tourmaline

Color: Black.

Healing and Spiritual Uses: For ancestral communication, working with the shadow self, purification, protection. Repels negative energy, diffuses stress and tension, and boosts the immune system.

Bloodstone

Color: Deep or dark green with red inclusions in the form of flecks, or spots.

Healing and Spiritual Uses: Type of quartz beneficial for creativity, strength, vitality, circulation, building energy, higher knowledge, courage, purification, detoxification, divination, weather prediction, shrinking tumors, and strengthening the heart.

Calcite

Color: Shades of gold, white, black, green, gray, yellow, blue, brown, and red.

Healing and Spiritual Uses: All-around healing stone, place in bath water as a healing and calming essence. Use for mental clarity, boosting memory, adjusting to transition, transforming negativity, learning, meditation, concentration, and astral projection.

Carnelian

Color: Translucent or clear, dark red or orange-red to reddish brown, gold-red, and brown.

Healing and Spiritual Uses: A kind of chalcedony excellent for enhancing sexuality, accessing fire energy, building power, motivation, activating energy and creativity. Helpful for past life awareness, fertility, purification, lower back problems, prosperity, protection against injury or falling, courage, mental focus, and strength.

Chrysocolla

Color: Blue and green, resembles turquoise.

Healing and Spiritual Uses: For tapping into your inner voice, sacred communication, digestion, ulcers, arthritis, hypertension, stress. Beneficial for self-confidence and musical ability.

Chrysoprase

Color: Apple-green, bright green.

Healing and Spiritual Uses: Quartz excellent for humility, personal insight, adapting to new environments or situations, creativity, fertility, and mental wellness. Relieves gout, strengthens eyesight, aids in cultivating the art of invisibility, out-of-body experience, psychonavigation, and shapeshifting.

Citrine

Color: Gold, brown-gold, pale to dark golden-yellow.

Healing and Spiritual Uses: Enhances mindfulness, intellectual reasoning, mental quickness, clarity. Relieves headaches, increases motivation, dispels negativity. Beneficial for manifesting goals and ideas, insight, personal empowerment.

Clear Quartz, Rock Quartz

Color: Clear, with or without inclusions.

Healing and Spiritual Uses: Called "the stars within the earth"; excellent for healing, doubling out (see "Amethyst"), balancing energy, sight, clarity, higher consciousness, spiritual enlightenment, meditation, divine guidance, perseverance, scientific applications, storing, releasing and regulating energy, purifying, unblocking energy in the body, mind, and spirit.

Diamond

Color: Clear, refracting all of the colors of the rainbow.

Healing and Spiritual Uses: Associated with lightning; the hardest substance of nature; used for healing, strength, power, good fortune, sexuality, love, insight, inspiration, protection, personal development, catalyzing and amplifying energy, multidimensional awareness, clarity, endurance, memory, and prosperity. Amplifies the energy of the wearer, be it positive or negative.

Emerald

Color: Light to deep green, and all shades in between.

Healing and Spiritual Uses: A kind of beryl excellent for psychic clarity, divination, growth, enhancing sexuality, healing, inspiration, cleansing, gastric problems, cultivating patience, equilibrium of body, mind, and spirit, meditation, wisdom, managing diabetes, back problems, and neutralizing radioactivity. Boosts the immune system and raises consciousness.

Fluorite

Color: Translucent in shades of blue, purple, pink, red, white, brown, yellow, gold, or colorless.

Healing and Spiritual Uses: For self-discipline, harmony, balance, empowering female energy, other world experience, cancer remission, arthritis, enhancing sexuality, spiritual awakening, out-of-body experience, projecting a sense of peace and tranquillity. Benefits teeth and bones.

Garnet, Almandine, Pyrope, Rhodolite

Color: Deep red translucent to deep emerald green, shades of yellow and brown.

Healing and Spiritual Uses: Employed for prosperity, physical strength, love, passion, imagination, flow of ideas, friendship, and creativity. Benefits the circulatory system. Helpful for accessing past life and future life experience, good luck in business, cultivating compassion, calming anger, and sharpening perceptions.

Hematite (Iron Oxide)

Color: Steel gray to iron black, sometimes with red spots.

Healing and Spiritual Uses: Excellent for grounding, enhancing the circulation of bodily fluids, manifesting light and energy, protection, astral projection, strength, and working with the shadow self. Boosts low self-esteem. Helpful for kidney problems, tissue regeneration, headaches, hysteria, and feelings of vulnerability.

Herkimer Diamond

Color: Clear, sometimes with tiny black specks on surface.

Healing and Spiritual Uses: Propitious for dreaming, higher love, stimulating psychic centers, and empowerment. Reduces stress, provides a natural filter for negativity, and assists in recalling past-life experience.

Jade, Jadeite, Nephrite, Serpentine

Color: Green, yellow, orange, blue, pink, red, lavender, white, brown.

Healing and Spiritual Uses: Considered the concentrated essence of love, beneficial for protection, divine love, connection with Earth, removal of toxins, purity, calming nerves, ridding yourself of negativity, developing the capacity for receiving and giving love, meditation, and spiritual awareness. Helpful for kidney and bladder disorders, and assists in childbirth.

Jasper

Color: Red, yellow, gold, brown, green, variegated and mottled.

Healing and Spiritual Uses: Member of Chalcedony family excellent for gem essences, endurance, cleansing, fortitude, prayer, protection, quick thinking, and neutralizing stress.

Kunzite

Color: Pink and pink-white.

Healing and Spiritual Uses: Stone with high lithium content beneficial for mental disorders, circulatory system, receiving love, joy, building tolerance and gratitude, releasing old hurts and unwanted memories, and balancing mental and emotional bodies.

Labradorite, Spectrolite

Color: Blue.

Healing and Spiritual Uses: A kind of feldspar employed in magic, ritual, and ceremony. Elevates consciousness, enhances psychic ability, and assists in regeneration, sexuality, and protection. Helpful in psychonavigation and shapeshifting, and divine communication.

Lapis Lazuli

Color: Deep blue, often with flecks of pyrite or mottled with white calcite.

Healing and Spiritual Uses: For psychic development, divination, protection, self-knowledge, wisdom, creativity, magical power, prosperity, doubling out (see "Amethyst"), shielding, and shapeshifting. A thought amplifier, helpful for respiratory or nervous disorders. Boosts energy and the immune system, expands awareness, and is propitious for personal empowerment.

Lepidolite

Color: purple, some with pink tourmaline crystals.

Healing and Spiritual Uses: Called the "stone of peace" and rich in lithium, excellent for out-of-body experience, increasing psychic ability, acceptance, awareness, peace and tranquillity, relieving stress, soothing anger and diffusing negativity, good luck, restful sleep, and pleasant dreams.

Malachite

Color: Bright green to light green, variegated.

Healing and Spiritual Uses: For magic, will-power, communication with nature, visions, rapport with animal kingdom, shapeshifting, moving energy, sound sleep, divine communication, and balance. Used for tissue regeneration and healing. Stimulates the optic nerve, balances dyslexia, and neutralizes radioactivity.

Moldavite

Color: Deep green.

Healing and Spiritual Uses: For transformation, shapeshifting, personal metamorphosis, cleansing, and personal attunement. Stimulates psychic senses, accelerates spiritual growth and development, and encourages motivation and change.

Moonstone

Color: Milky and translucent, pale blue, green, and gray.

Healing and Spiritual Uses: Connection to female energy, receptivity, tidal flow, cycles, multidimensional awareness. Beneficial for balancing emotions, the reproductive organs, and healing. Enhances sensitivity, intuition, clairvoyance, open-mindedness. Employed in farming, divination, artistic pursuits, and dancing. Brings good fortune, fruitfulness, and true love.

Obsidian, Apache Tear

Color: Black transparent or semi-transparent, flecked with white or striped.

Healing and Spiritual Uses: Volcanic stone for protection and working with the shadow self. Sharpens inner and outer vision. Used for divination (obsidian mirrors), ritual tools, past life regression, good luck, letting go of old patterns and memories, and in ceremony and ritual.

Onyx

Color: Black, white, or translucent, with layers of red, yellow, brown, or pink.

Healing and Spiritual Uses: Story-telling stone, beneficial for building life patterns, creating structure in your life, accessing physical memories, and alleviating mental and emotional stress. Strengthens energy, lessens fear and worry, and allows for communication with underworld energies.

Opal, Fire Opal, Star Opal

Color: Milky or white with multicolored patterns inside, opaque, clear, transparent, yellow-brown.

Healing and Spiritual Uses: Containing up to 30 percent water and called the "eye stone," excellent for harmonizing energy, eye disorders, accessing cosmic energy, activating creativity and wisdom, gaining balance and inspiration, doubling out (see "Amethyst"), intensifying emotional states, business, protection, and lucid dreaming.

Peridot

Color: Clear, pale green.

Healing and Spiritual Uses: For balancing energy, emotional tranquillity, healing, insight, clairvoyance, personal empowerment, vision, clarity of purpose, and enlightenment. Enhances digestion, stimulates tissue regeneration, and boosts confidence.

Rhodochrosite

Color: Orange and pink with white veins or stripes.

Healing and Spiritual Uses: Employed in matters of the heart, and accessing your inner child. Helpful for asthma, respiratory illness, kidney disorders, and alleviating irrational fears and worries. Enhances dreaming and promotes restful sleep.

Rose Quartz

Color: Light to medium pink mottled with white.

Healing and Spiritual Uses: Excellent for emotional balancing in relationships, friendships, and higher love. Helpful for spiritual awakening, compassion, personal attunement, forgiveness, self-acceptance, adapting to changes, tapping into the inner voice, restoring faith, and fertility. Raises low self-esteem, assists in healing, and enhances creativity.

Ruby

Color: Deep red to bright purple-red, shades of pink and lavender.

Healing and Spiritual Uses: Builds inner strength, amplifies inner energy, enhances personal empowerment, insight, creativity, physical and mental strength, and activates the life force. Beneficial for building energy and drive. Aids the heart and circulatory system, and is excellent for doubling out (see "Amethyst"), clarity, friendship, passion, and protection.

Rutilated Quartz, Venus Hair, Fleches d'Amour

Color: Clear to pale yellow with needlelike rutile inclusions.

Healing and Spiritual Uses: For healing, directing energy, balance, insight, sustaining good health, and creating positive life patterns. Boosts the immune system, elevates energy, enhances sexuality and self-esteem.

Sapphire, Star Sapphire

Color: Deep blue, shades of black, gray, green, and yellow, star sapphire with aqueous inclusions, which create a five-pointed star on the stone's surface.

Healing and Spiritual Uses: For psychic development, enhancing focus, creativity, providing serenity, calming emotions, diffusing negativity, healing, especially eyesight, easing stress and tension, and dispelling fear. Excellent for concentration, meditation, divine communication, divination, doubling out (see "Amethyst"), astral projection, aligning body, mind, and spirit, and good fortune.

Smithsonite

Color: Shades of pink, purple, blue, yellow, and green.

Healing and Spiritual Uses: Named for James Smithson, founder of the Smithsonian Institute, beneficial for healing, enhancing relationships, sexuality, unity, evoking emotion, and sparking romance. Strengthens feelings of security and clarity. Accesses innovative thoughts, ideas, and multidimensional awareness.

Smoky Quartz

Color: Medium to dark brown and chocolate brown-black.

Healing and Spiritual Uses: For grounding, centering, connecting to the Earth, healing, and building prosperity. Neutralizes negative influences and balances the nervous system. Helpful for radiation-related illnesses. Used for crystal scrying.

Sodalite

Color: Blue, sometimes with gray or white veins.

Healing and Spiritual Uses: Helpful for lymph circulation, mental clarity, and boosting the immune system. Enhances objectivity, vision, clairvoyance, balances the metabolism, and neutralizes radiation.

Sugilite

Color: Purple, sometimes with darker veins.

Healing and Spiritual Uses: Employed in dreaming, divine communication, channeling, out-of-body experience, multidimensional awareness and travel. Enhances psychic abilities and helps to charge the energy body.

Tanzanite

Color: Clear, shades of blue and purple-blue.

Healing and Spiritual Uses: Excellent for insight and helpful for discerning the truth. Used in divination, channeling, divine communication, astral projection, and psychonavigation. Enhances psychic abilities and expands perception.

Tiger's Eye, Cat's Eye

Color: Light to dark brown with fibrous inclusions.

Healing and Spiritual Uses: Quartz stone used for balance, invisibility, strength, insight, and inner knowledge. Instills the confidence to accomplish your goals and recognize inner resources. Helpful for protection, mental focus, concentration, and shapeshifting.

Topaz

Color: Bright yellow, brown-yellow, shades of green, blue, and brown.

Healing and Spiritual Uses: Enhances insight, knowledge, intention, loyalty, higher love, and creativity. Helpful in unmasking deception in others, recharging energy, balancing and warming, healing, problem solving, and scientific discovery. Assists in artistic pursuits, calms the nerves, eases tension, and is excellent in gem essences, or for treating eyesight problems.

Tourmaline

Color: Green, pink to salmon (rubelite), blue, opalized.

Healing and Spiritual Uses: Strengthens energy body and boosts the immune system. Used for regeneration, creativity, and growth.

Beneficial cleansing and purifying properties for the body that are helpful in polarity work and healing. Employed for divine communication and spiritual awakening.

Turquoise

Color: Sky blue to soft and deep green or green-blue.

Healing and Spiritual Uses: Excellent for ritual and ceremony, for gaining wholeness, knowledge, elemental wisdom, communicating with devas and ancestors, and promoting personal attunement. Stimulates motivation and healing. Beneficial for respiratory problems, greater self-realization, and endurance.

Watermelon Tourmaline, Rainbow Tourmaline

Color: Multicolored bands of pink, green, and purple.

Healing and Spiritual Uses: For inner peace, harmony, balancing and energizing body, mind, and spirit, polarity work, and problem-solving.

Zircon

Color: Clear in shades of blue, green, yellow, red, and brown.

Healing and Spiritual Uses: A look-alike for diamond, excellent for personal reflection, calming nerves, teaching patience and reserve, and improving tolerance.

BOOKS BY THE CROSSING PRESS

Pocket Guide to Acupressure Points for Women
ISBN 0-89594-879-6

Pocket Guide to Aromatherapy
ISBN 0-89594-815-X

Pocket Guide to Astrology
ISBN 0-89594-820-6

Pocket Guide to Ayurvedic Healing
ISBN 0-89594-764-1

Pocket Guide to Bach Flower Essences
ISBN 0-89594-865-6

Pocket Guide to Celtic Spirituality
ISBN 0-89594-907-5

Pocket Guide to Chakras
ISBN 0-89594-949-0

Pocket Guide to Fortunetelling
ISBN 0-89594-875-3

Pocket Guide to Hatha Yoga
ISBN 0-89594-911-3

Pocket Guide to Herbal First Aid
ISBN 0-89594-967-9

Pocket Guide to Meditation
ISBN 0-89594-886-9

Pocket Guide to Naturopathic Medicine
ISBN 0-89594-821-4

Pocket Guide to Numerology
ISBN 0-89594-826-5

Pocket Guide to Self Hypnosis
ISBN 0-89594-824-9

Pocket Guide to Shamanism
ISBN 0-89594-845-1

Pocket Guide to The Tarot
ISBN 0-89594-822-2

Pocket Guide to Visualization
ISBN 0-89594-885-0

Pocket Guide to Wicca
ISBN 0-89594-904-0

Pocket Herbal Reference Guide
ISBN 0-89594-568-1

09474>

7 42851 00695 3